TASTE OF
THAILAND

Taste of
THAILAND

70 SIMPLE-TO-COOK RECIPES

KIT CHAN

SMITHMARK

This edition published in 1996 by
SMITHMARK Publishers
a division of U.S. Media Holdings, Inc.
16 East 32nd Street
New York
NY 10016

SMITHMARK books are available for bulk purchase for sales promotion
and premium use. For details write or call the Manager of Special Sales,
SMITHMARK Publishers
a division of U.S. Media Holdings, Inc.
16 East 32nd Street
New York
NY 10016
(212) 532 - 6600

ISBN 0 7651 9878 9

Publisher: Joanna Lorenz
Senior Cookery Editor: Linda Fraser
Cookery Editor: Maggie Mayhew
Designer: Alan Marshall
Photography and styling: Thomas Odulate
Illustrator: Madeleine David

Printed in Singapore by Star Standard Industries Pte Ltd.

10 9 8 7 6 5 4 3 2 1

CONTENTS

INTRODUCTION

Thailand is probably one of the most diverse and complex countries in Asia. Geographically it is halfway between India and China and so it is hardly surprising that the cultures of its neighbors have influenced the development of its national cuisine.

Thailand is divided into five regions that have distinct geographical and cultural differences; from dense jungles and mountainous retreats to vast plains of paddy-fields, and from untamed rivers to brilliant white sandy beaches and the warm clear ocean.

The climate is tropical so there is an abundance of fruit, vegetables and flowers. The carving of fruits and vegetables into exotic sculptures, decorated with flowers and foliage, has become an art form in Thailand. The country also boasts over one thousand varieties of orchids and the orchid has become a national emblem.

The cooking is a source of pride and wonder. Thai cooks will always strive for a balance of flavor, texture and color in a dish. Presentation varies from simple plastic bowls at sidewalk stalls to beautifully decorated china and artistic displays in the finer restaurants, but the complexity of taste and flavor in their culinary magic is consistent.

The most prevalent flavor in Thai cooking comes from the chili, which surprisingly was introduced to the country by Portuguese missionaries in the sixteenth century. It didn't take the Thais long to make good use of it, believing that chilies cool the body, stimulate the appetite and bring balance and harmony to their food.

Food is a celebration. To have to eat alone ranks high on the Thai scale of misfortunes. A Thai meal offers a combination of flavors: sweet, hot, sour, salty and sometimes bitter. Usually, in addition to the obligatory bowl of rice, there will be a variety of dishes including a soup, a curry, a steamed dish, a fried one, a salad and one or two sauces. The portion size will depend on the number of people eating. All the dishes are placed on the table at the same time and shared. They are not eaten in any particular order.

Water and tea are the most common liquid accompaniments served with a meal. Thai whiskey is often drunk at festive gatherings.

Below: Thai villages nestle in the lush and beautiful countryside, where the occupants grow a wide range of fresh fruits and vegetables. These people usually sell their goods at one of the many markets.

In days gone by, Thais ate with their fingers, pressing rice into small balls, which were then dipped into other dishes. Today, Thais eat with a large spoon to scoop up sauces and a fork to mix and push food on to the spoon. Knives are rarely used because meat is usually served in small pieces and chopsticks are only used to eat Chinese-style noodles.

Thais tend to cook by "feel," taking into account the tastes and preferences of their family. You should always taste and adjust the seasoning to your own taste. If you find something is too salty or too sweet and, even more importantly, if you are not used to the hotness of chilies, add a little at a time until you get a balance that you like. In short, Thai cuisine is light and fresh with delicately balanced spices and a harmony of flavors, colors and textures designed to appeal to both the eyes and the palate.

Above: floating markets are a typical sight throughout the Thai islands, where the freshest of produce can be bought.

EQUIPMENT

You don't need special equipment to produce a Thai meal. In fact, you will probably have most of the things already. The basic items are listed below.

A sturdy chopping board with a cleaver or a large chef's knife to use for the heavy cutting and chopping, and a small paring knife for the little jobs.

A wok is essential – for most meals this is the only type of pan you will need. Perfect for stir-frying, cooking curries and simmering dishes as well as for deep-frying and steaming.

A large steamer basket is useful. The most common are those made of bamboo that can be purchased quite cheaply from Oriental stores.

A large granite or heavy mortar and pestle for grinding spices and pounding curry paste to give the sort of texture required for Thai food. Although a coffee grinder or blender can be used instead, do bear in mind that the pungent flavors may linger.

If you eat rice regularly, think about investing in an electric rice cooker. It does the job well, frees up the stovetop and, best of all, it makes burnt rice pans a thing of the past.

Equipment (clockwise from top): two-tier bamboo steamer, large granite mortar and pestle, wooden chopping board with cleaver, large chef's knife and small paring knife, a wire basket draining spoon and wok.

INGREDIENTS

BAMBOO SHOOTS

The edible young shoots of the bamboo plant. Pale to bright yellow when fresh. Fresh shoots need some preparation and take quite a long time to cook. When buying canned shoots, look for whole ones as they are generally better than ready-sliced.

Clockwise from top left: green eggplant, yellow eggplant, pea eggplant and purple eggplant.

BANANA LEAVES

Glossy, dark green leaves of the banana tree, are used to line steamers or to wrap foods such as chicken or fish prior to broiling or baking. They impart a vague flavor of fine tea.

BASIL

A pungent herb much used in the Mediterranean regions and in South-East Asia. Three varieties of basil are used in Thai cooking – *bai mangluk* (hairy basil), *bai horapa* (sweet basil) and *bai grapao* (Thai or Holy basil). Thai basil tastes hot and slightly medicinal. *Bai horapa* is the most popular. It has small, dark leaves with reddish-purple stems and flowers. Its flavor is reminiscent of anise and fairly strong.

BEAN CURD OR TOFU

Most often used in soups and Chinese dishes. It is made from soy beans and is rich in vitamins and minerals. It is usually sold in square blocks packed in water. Bean curd or tofu comes in many forms – fresh, fried and dried.

BEAN SAUCE

Made from salted, fermented soy beans, this sauce is a popular flavoring agent in a variety of Asian dishes. It is also known as yellow bean sauce.

BEAN SPROUTS

Sprouted from mung beans, bean sprouts are used in all sorts of salads and stir-fried dishes. Rich in vitamins, protein and iron, bean sprouts are widely available in supermarkets. Look for crisp, firm, fresh-looking sprouts with little scent.

CHILI

There are many different kinds of chilies. The small, red and green fresh chilies, known as Thai or bird's eye, are extremely hot. Larger varieties are slightly milder. The "fire" comes from the seeds so discard them if a milder flavor is preferred. Chilies contain volatile oil that can irritate the skin and cause eyes to burn. Wear rubber gloves while you chop or seed chilies, or wash your hands immediately after preparing them.

COCONUT MILK (UNSWEETENED)

This unsweetened liquid is made from a mixture of grated coconut flesh and water. Coconut milk is an essential ingredient of many Thai dishes. It is available in compressed blocks, cans or in powder form.

Clockwise from top left: Thai or Holy basil, lemon basil and hairy basil.

Left: fresh drained tofu; right: fried tofu cubes.

CORIANDER AND CILANTRO

The leaves, called cilantro, and seeds of the coriander plant are essential in Thai cooking. The root is also used to make a marinade.

CURRY PASTE

This is traditionally made by pounding together fresh herbs and spices. There are several different kinds. Homemade curry pastes take time to prepare but keep well. Store-bought pastes are a good alternative.

Clockwise from top: green chilies, Thai orange chilies, Indian chilies, red chilies, and mild green chilies.

EGGPLANT

A vegetable with a mildly sweet flavor. Many varieties of eggplant are used in Thai cooking, from tiny pea eggplant, which are added just before the end of cooking, to white, yellow or green ones. When these are unavailable, you can substitute the purple variety.

FISH SAUCE (NAM PLA)
The most commonly used flavoring in Thai food. Fish sauce is used in the same way soy sauce is used in Chinese dishes. It is made from salted anchovies and has a strong salty flavor.

GALANGAL
A member of the ginger family, also known as *kha* or *laos*, that looks similar to fresh ginger, but with a more translucent skin and a pinkish tinge. It has a wonderful sharp, lemony taste and it is prepared in a similar fashion to ginger. Best used fresh, it is also available dried or in powder form.

Clockwise from top left: pickled garlic, fresh ginger, fresh turmeric, fresh garlic, galangal root.

GARLIC
Garlic is indispensable in Thai cooking. Heads of the Asian variety are quite small. Look out for fresh shiny heads of garlic with no soft, dusty or moldy cloves. Jars of pickled garlic can be bought from Asian stores.

GINGER
A root of Chinese and Indian origin. It is always used fresh rather than dried and should be peeled and chopped or crushed before cooking. It is available in supermarkets. Look for shiny fat roots that aren't wrinkled or shriveled. Though not used as frequently as galangal in Thai cooking, ginger makes a good alternative.

KAFFIR LIME
This is similar to the common lime but has a knobbly skin. The zest of the fruit is often used and the dark glossy green leaves from the tree impart a pungent lemony-lime flavor to soups, curries and other dishes. You can buy them fresh in Asian stores. They keep well and can be frozen. Dried kaffir limes are also available.

LEMONGRASS
Also known as citronella, lemongrass has long pale green stalks and a bulbous end similar to a spring onion. Only the bottom 5 inches is used. It has a woody texture and an aromatic lemony scent. Unless finely chopped, it is always removed before serving because it is so fibrous.

PALM SUGAR
Strongly flavored, hard brown sugar made from the sap of the coconut palm tree. Available in Asian stores. If you have trouble finding it, use dark brown sugar instead.

ROASTED GROUND RICE
Raw glutinous rice grains are dry-fried until brown, then ground to a powder. A traditional ingredient in salads.

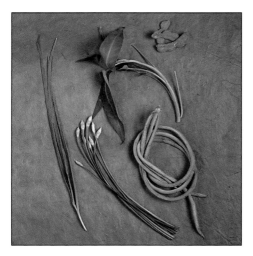

Clockwise from top left: water spinach, taramind pods, snake beans, garlic shoots and garlic chives.

Clockwise from top: lemongrass, Thai shallots, kaffir limes and fresh kaffir lime leaves.

SALTED EGGS
A traditional way of preserving duck eggs in Asia. You can find them in most Asian stores, often sold covered in a thick layer of charcoal-grey ash. Rub off the ash with your finger under running water and then hard-cook the eggs.

SHALLOTS
Thai shallots have a lovely pinkish-purple colour and are used extensively in Thai cuisine instead of onions.

SOY SAUCE
Made from fermented soybeans, soy sauce is available in light or dark versions and can be quite salty. It is the background seasoning to many stir-fried and noodle dishes.

TAMARIND
An acidic tropical fruit that resembles a bean pod. It is usually sold dried or pulped. To make tamarind juice, take 2 tablespoons of tamarind or about 2 stock cube-size pieces and leave to soak in $\frac{2}{3}$ cup of warm water for about 10 minutes. Squeeze out as much tamarind juice as possible by pressing all the liquid through a strainer and use as in the recipes.

VINEGAR
Thais use a mild, plain white vinegar. Cider or Japanese rice wine vinegar can be used instead.

SNACKS AND APPETIZERS

Food and snacking are inescapable parts of life in Bangkok. Indeed, throughout the whole of Thailand a constant supply of spicy titbits are available at roadside stalls and market places.

The variety of snacks is huge. Some dishes are small, such as savory pastries, spring rolls, steamed dumplings and rice balls. Others, such as noodle dishes, are more substantial and can be a meal in themselves. These snacks are not considered real food in Asia, but merely an enjoyable way to relax during any spare time, a nibble between meals or a treat at the market.

Appetizers as such are not common in a Thai meal as all the dishes are brought to the table at once. The dishes in this chapter will serve well as a snack at cocktail parties or as part of a main meal, but will also be excellent appetizers if you wish to serve them as a separate course.

Rice Cakes with Spicy Dipping Sauce

Rice cakes are a classic Thai appetizer. They are easy to make and can be kept in an airtight box almost indefinitely.

INGREDIENTS

Serves 4–6
1 cup jasmine rice
1½ cups water
oil for frying and greasing

For the spicy dipping sauce
6–8 dried chilies
½ teaspoon salt
2 shallots, chopped
2 garlic cloves, chopped
4 cilantro roots
10 white peppercorns
1 cup unsweetened coconut milk
1 teaspoon shrimp paste
4 ounces ground pork
4 ounces cherry tomatoes, chopped
1 tablespoon fish sauce
1 tablespoon palm sugar
2 tablespoons tamarind juice
2 tablespoons coarsely chopped
  roasted peanuts
2 scallions, finely chopped

1 Stem the chilies and remove most of the seeds. Soak the chilies in warm water for 20 minutes. Drain and transfer to a mortar.

2 Add the salt and grind with a pestle until the chilies are crushed. Add the shallots, garlic, cilantro roots and peppercorns. Pound together until you have a coarse paste.

3 Pour the coconut milk into a saucepan and boil until it begins to separate. Add the pounded chili paste. Cook for 2–3 minutes, until it is fragrant. Stir in the shrimp paste. Cook for another minute.

4 Add the pork, stirring to break up any lumps. Cook for about 5–10 minutes. Add the tomatoes, fish sauce, palm sugar and tamarind juice. Simmer until the sauce thickens.

5 Stir in the chopped peanuts and scallions. Remove from the heat and set aside to cool.

6 Wash the rice in several changes of water. Put in a saucepan, add the water and cover with a tight-fitting lid. Bring to a boil, reduce the heat and simmer gently for about 15 minutes.

7 Remove the lid and fluff up the rice. Turn out on to a lightly greased tray and press down with the back of a large spoon. Set aside to dry out overnight in a very low oven, until it is completely dry and firm.

8 Remove the rice from the tray and break into bite-size pieces. Heat the oil in a wok or deep-fat fryer.

9 Deep-fry the rice cakes in batches for about 1 minute, until they puff up, taking care not to brown them too much. Remove and drain. Serve accompanied with the dipping sauce.

Spring Rolls

These crunchy spring rolls are as popular in Thai cuisine as they are in the Chinese. Thais fill their version with a garlic, pork and noodle filling.

INGREDIENTS

Makes about 24
4–6 dried Chinese mushrooms, soaked
2 ounces bean thread noodles, soaked
2 tablespoons vegetable oil
2 garlic cloves, chopped
2 red chilies, seeded and chopped
8 ounces ground pork
2 ounces chopped cooked shrimp
2 tablespoons fish sauce
1 teaspoon sugar
1 carrot, finely shredded
2 ounces bamboo shoots, chopped
¼ cup bean sprouts
2 scallions, chopped
1 tablespoon chopped cilantro
2 tablespoons flour
24 × 6-inch square spring roll wrappers
freshly ground black pepper
oil for frying

1 Drain and chop the mushrooms. Drain the noodles and cut into short lengths of about 2 inches.

2 Heat the oil in a wok or frying pan, add the garlic and chilies and fry for 30 seconds. Add the pork, stirring until the meat is browned.

3 Add the noodles, mushrooms and shrimp. Season with fish sauce, sugar and pepper. Turn into a bowl.

4 Mix in the carrot, bamboo shoots, bean sprouts, scallions and chopped cilantro for the filling.

5 Put the flour in a small bowl and mix with a little water to make a paste. Place a spoonful of filling in the center of a spring roll wrapper.

6 Turn the bottom edge over to cover the filling, then fold in the left and right sides. Roll the wrapper up almost to the top edge. Brush the top edge with flour paste and seal. Repeat with the rest of the wrappers.

7 Heat the oil in a wok or deep-fat fryer. Slide in the spring rolls a few at a time and fry until crisp and golden brown. Remove with a slotted spoon and drain on paper towels. Serve hot with Thai sweet chili sauce to dip them into, if you like.

Pork Satay

Originating in Indonesia, satay are skewers of meat marinated with spices and grilled quickly over charcoal. It's street food at its best, prepared by vendors with portable grills who set up stalls at every street corner and market place. As well as pork, you can also make satay with chicken, beef or lamb. Serve with satay sauce and cucumber relish.

INGREDIENTS

Makes about 20

1 pound lean pork
1 teaspoon grated ginger
1 lemongrass stalk, finely chopped
3 garlic cloves, finely chopped
1 tablespoon medium curry paste
1 teaspoon ground cumin
1 teaspoon ground turmeric
4 tablespoons coconut cream
2 tablespoons fish sauce
1 teaspoon sugar
20 wooden satay skewers
oil for cooking

For the satay sauce

1 cup unsweetened coconut milk
2 tablespoons red curry paste
½ cup crunchy peanut butter
½ cup chicken stock
3 tablespoons brown sugar
2 tablespoons tamarind juice
1 tablespoon fish sauce
1 teaspoon salt

1 Cut the pork thinly into 2-inch strips. Mix together the ginger, lemongrass, garlic, medium curry paste, cumin, turmeric, coconut cream, fish sauce and sugar.

2 Pour over the pork and set aside to marinate for about 2 hours.

3 Meanwhile, make the sauce. Heat the coconut milk over a medium heat, then add the red curry paste, peanut butter, chicken stock and sugar.

4 Cook and stir until smooth, about 5–6 minutes. Add the tamarind juice, fish sauce and salt to taste.

5 Thread the meat onto skewers. Brush with oil and grill over charcoal or under a preheated broiler for 3–4 minutes on each side, turning occasionally, until cooked and golden brown. Serve with the satay sauce.

Lacy Duck Egg Nets

You can find duck eggs in good Asian supermarkets or order them direct from farms, but regular eggs are also good here. Thais have a special dispenser to make the net, but you can use a pastry bag fitted with a small nozzle or a squeeze bottle.

INGREDIENTS

Makes about 12–15
For the filling
4 cilantro roots
2 garlic cloves
10 white peppercorns
pinch of salt
3 tablespoons oil
1 small onion, finely chopped
4 ounces lean ground pork
3 ounces shelled shrimp, chopped
½ cup roasted peanuts, ground
1 teaspoon palm sugar
fish sauce, to taste

For the egg nets
6 duck eggs or jumbo hen eggs
cilantro leaves, to serve, plus extra
  to garnish
scallion tassels and sliced red chillies,
  to garnish

1 Using a mortar and pestle, grind the cilantro roots, garlic, white peppercorns and salt into a paste.

2 Heat 2 tablespoons of the oil, add the paste and fry until fragrant. Add the onion and cook until softened. Add the pork and shrimp and continue to stir-fry until the meat is cooked.

3 Add the peanuts, palm sugar, salt and fish sauce, to taste. Stir the mixture and continue to cook until it becomes a little sticky. Remove from the heat. Transfer the mixture to a bowl and set aside.

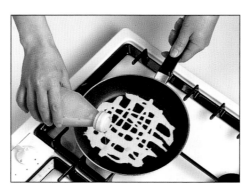

4 Break the eggs into a bowl, and beat with a fork. Grease a non-stick frying pan with the remaining oil and heat. Using a special dispenser or a suitable alternative, trail the eggs across the pan to make a net pattern, about 5 inches in diameter.

5 When the net is set, carefully remove it from the pan, and repeat until all the eggs have been used up.

6 To assemble, lay a net on a board, lay a few cilantro leaves on it and top with a spoonful of filling. Turn in the edges to make a neat square shape. Repeat with the rest of the nets. Arrange on a serving dish and garnish with the fresh cilantro leaves, scallion tassels and chilies.

Son-in-law Eggs

This fascinating name comes from a story about a prospective bridegroom who wanted to impress his future mother-in-law and devised a recipe from the only other dish he knew how to make – cooked eggs. The hard-cooked eggs are deep fried and then drenched with a sweet, piquant tamarind sauce.

INGREDIENTS

Serves 4–6

scant ½ cup palm sugar
5 tablespoons fish sauce
6 tablespoons tamarind juice
oil for frying
6 shallots, finely sliced
6 garlic cloves, finely sliced
6 red chilies, sliced
6 hard-cooked eggs, shelled
lettuce, to serve
sprigs of cilantro, to garnish

1 Combine the palm sugar, fish sauce and tamarind juice in a small saucepan. Bring to a boil, stirring until the sugar dissolves, then simmer for about 5 minutes.

2 Taste and add more palm sugar, fish sauce or tamarind juice, if necessary. It should be sweet, salty and slightly sour. Transfer the sauce to a bowl and set aside.

3 Heat the oil in a wok or deep-fat fryer. Meanwhile, heat a couple of spoonfuls of the oil in a frying pan and fry the shallots, garlic and chilies until golden brown. Transfer the mixture to a bowl and set aside.

4 Deep-fry the eggs in the oil for about 3–5 minutes, until golden brown. Remove and drain on paper towels. Cut the eggs in quarters and arrange on a bed of lettuce. Drizzle with the sauce and sprinkle over the shallots. Garnish with sprigs of cilantro.

Fried Clams with Chili and Yellow Bean Sauce

Seafood is abundant in Thailand, especially at all of the beach holiday resorts. This delicious dish, which is simple to prepare, is one of the favorites.

INGREDIENTS

Serves 4–6

2¼ pounds fresh clams
2 tablespoons vegetable oil
4 garlic cloves, finely chopped
1 tablespoon grated ginger
4 shallots, finely chopped
2 tablespoons yellow bean sauce
6 red chilies, seeded and chopped
1 tablespoon fish sauce
pinch of sugar
handful of basil leaves, plus extra
   to garnish

1 Wash and scrub the clams. Heat the oil in a wok or large frying pan. Add the garlic and ginger and fry for 30 seconds, add the shallots and fry for another minute.

2 Add the clams. Using a fish slice or spatula, turn them a few times to coat with the oil. Add the yellow bean sauce and half the red chilies.

3 Continue to cook, stirring often, for about 5–7 minutes until all the clams open. You may need to add a splash of water. Adjust the seasoning with fish sauce and a little sugar.

4 Finally add the basil and transfer to individual bowls or a platter. Garnish with the remaining red chilies and basil leaves.

Pan-steamed Mussels with Thai Herbs

Another simple dish to prepare. The lemongrass adds a refreshing tang to the mussels.

INGREDIENTS

Serves 4–6
2¼ pounds mussels, cleaned and
 beards removed
2 lemongrass stalks, finely chopped
4 shallots, chopped
4 kaffir lime leaves, coarsely torn
2 red chilies, sliced
1 tablespoon fish sauce
2 tablespoons lime juice
2 scallions, chopped, to garnish
cilantro leaves, to garnish

1 Place all the ingredients, except for the scallions and cilantro, in a large saucepan and stir thoroughly.

2 Cover and steam for 5–7 minutes, shaking the saucepan occasionally, until the mussels open. Discard any mussels that remain closed.

3 Transfer the cooked mussels to a serving platter.

4 Garnish the mussels with chopped scallions and cilantro leaves. Serve the dish immediately.

Fish Cakes with Cucumber Relish

These wonderful small fish cakes are a very familiar and popular appetizer. They are usually accompanied by Thai beer.

INGREDIENTS

Makes about 12

11 ounces white fish fillet, such as cod, cut into chunks
2 tablespoons red curry paste
1 egg
2 tablespoons fish sauce
1 teaspoon sugar
2 tablespoons cornstarch
3 kaffir lime leaves, shredded
1 tablespoon chopped cilantro
2 ounces green beans, finely sliced
oil for frying
Chinese mustard cress, to garnish

For the cucumber relish

4 tablespoons Thai coconut or rice vinegar
4 tablespoons water
4 tablespoons sugar
1 head pickled garlic
1 cucumber, quartered and sliced
4 shallots, finely sliced
1 tablespoon finely chopped ginger
2 red chilies, seeded and finely sliced

1 For the cucumber relish, bring the vinegar, water and sugar to a boil. Stir until the sugar dissolves, remove from the heat and cool.

2 Combine the rest of the relish ingredients together in a bowl and pour over the vinegar mixture.

3 Combine the fish, curry paste and egg in a food processor and process well. Transfer the mixture to a bowl, add the rest of the ingredients, except for the oil and garnish, and mix well.

4 Mold and shape the mixture into cakes about 2 inches in diameter and ¼ inch thick.

5 Heat the oil in a wok or deep-fat fryer. Fry the fish cakes, a few at a time, for about 4–5 minutes or until golden brown. Remove and drain on paper towels. Garnish with Chinese mustard cress and serve with the cucumber relish.

Crisp-fried Crab Claws

INGREDIENTS

Serves 4
8 tablespoons rice flour
1 tablespoon cornstarch
½ teaspoon sugar
1 egg
4 tablespoons cold water
1 lemongrass stalk, finely chopped
2 garlic cloves, finely chopped
1 tablespoon chopped cilantro
1–2 red chilies, seeded and chopped
1 teaspoon fish sauce
oil for frying
12 half-shelled crab claws
freshly ground black pepper

For the chili vinegar dip
3 tablespoons sugar
½ cup water
½ cup red wine vinegar
1 tablespoon fish sauce
2–4 red chilies, seeded and chopped

1 To make the chili dip, put the sugar and water in a saucepan and bring to a boil, stirring, until the sugar dissolves. Lower the heat and simmer for 5–7 minutes. Stir in the rest of the ingredients and set aside.

2 Combine the rice flour, cornstarch and sugar in a large bowl. Beat the egg with the cold water, then stir the liquid into the flour mixture and mix well until it forms a light batter.

3 Add the lemongrass, garlic, cilantro, red chilies, fish sauce and freshly ground black pepper.

4 Heat the oil in a wok or deep-fat fryer. Pat dry the crab claws with paper towels and dip one at a time in the batter. Gently drop the battered claws in the hot oil, a few at a time. Fry until golden brown. Drain on paper towels. Serve hot with the chili vinegar dip.

Golden Wonton Pouches

These crisp pouches are delicious served as an appetizer or to accompany drinks at a party.

INGREDIENTS

Makes about 20
4 ounces ground pork
4 ounces crab meat
2–3 wood ears, soaked and chopped
1 tablespoon chopped cilantro
1 teaspoon chopped garlic
2 tablespoons chopped scallion
1 egg
1 tablespoon fish sauce
1 teaspoon soy sauce
pinch of sugar
20 wonton wrappers
20 chives, blanched (optional)
oil for deep-frying
freshly ground black pepper
plum or sweet chili sauce, to serve

1 In a mixing bowl, combine the pork, crab meat, wood ears, cilantro, garlic, scallions and egg. Mix thoroughly and season with fish sauce, soy sauce, sugar and freshly ground black pepper.

2 Take a wonton wrapper and place it on a flat surface. Put a heaped teaspoonful of filling in the center of the wrapper, then pull up the edges of the pastry around the filling.

3 Pinch together to seal. If you like, you can go a step further and tie it with a long chive. Repeat with the remaining pork mixture.

4 Heat the oil in a wok or deep-fat fryer. Fry the wontons in batches until they are crisp and golden brown. Drain on paper towels and serve immediately with either a plum or sweet chili sauce.

Steamed Seafood Packages

Very neat and delicate, these make an excellent appetizer.

INGREDIENTS

Serves 4
8 ounces crab meat
2 ounces shelled shrimp, chopped
6 water chestnuts, chopped
2 tablespoons chopped bamboo shoots
1 tablespoon chopped scallions
1 teaspoon chopped ginger
1 tablespoon soy sauce
1 tablespoon fish sauce
12 rice sheets
banana leaves
oil for brushing
1 tablespoon soy sauce
2 scallions, shredded, to garnish
2 red chilies, seeded and sliced, and
  cilantro leaves, to garnish

1 Combine the crab meat, chopped shrimp, chestnuts, bamboo shoots, scallion and ginger in a bowl. Mix well, then add the soy sauce and fish sauce. Stir until blended.

2 Take a rice sheet and dip it in warm water. Place it on a flat surface and leave for a few seconds to soften.

--- COOK'S TIP ---

The seafood packages will spread out when steamed so be sure to space them well apart to prevent them sticking together.

3 Place a spoonful of the filling in the center of the sheet and fold into a square package. Repeat with the rest of the rice sheets and seafood mixture.

4 Line a steamer with banana leaves and brush them with oil. Put the packages, seam-side down, on the leaves and steam over high heat for 6–8 minutes, until the filling is cooked.

5 Transfer to a plate and garnish with the remaining ingredients.

Chicken and Sticky Rice Balls

These balls can either be steamed or deep-fried. The fried versions are crunchy and are excellent for serving at cocktail parties.

INGREDIENTS

Makes about 30
1 pound ground chicken
1 egg
1 teaspoon tapioca flour
4 scallions, finely chopped
2 tablespoons chopped cilantro
2 tablespoons fish sauce
pinch of sugar
8 ounces cooked sticky rice
banana leaves
oil for brushing
freshly ground black pepper
1 small carrot, shredded, to garnish
1 red bell pepper, to garnish
chopped chives, to garnish
sweet chili sauce, to serve

1 In a mixing bowl, combine the ground chicken, egg, tapioca flour, scallions and cilantro. Mix well and season with fish sauce, sugar and freshly ground black pepper.

2 Spread the cooked sticky rice on a plate or flat tray.

3 Place a teaspoonful of the chicken mixture on the bed of rice. With damp hands, roll and shape the mixture in the rice to make a ball about the size of a walnut. Repeat with the rest of the chicken mixture.

> ——— COOK'S TIP ———
>
> Sticky rice, also known as glutinous rice, has a very high gluten content. It is so called because the grains stick together when cooked. It can be eaten both as a savory and as a sweet dish.

4 Line a bamboo steamer with banana leaves and lightly brush them with oil. Place the chicken balls on the leaves, spacing well apart to prevent them sticking together. Steam over high heat for about 10 minutes or until cooked.

5 Remove and arrange on serving plates. Garnish with shredded carrots, strips of red pepper and chives. Serve with sweet chili sauce.

SOUPS

Soup is a very significant part of a Thai's daily fare. It can be served as a snack or a light lunch. A bowl of soup is nearly always included in a Thai meal. It is placed on the table alongside the other dishes, to be enjoyed a little at a time as a liquid refreshment. Thai soups, which are quick and easy to prepare, are usually based on a light broth and many of them are enriched with unsweetened coconut milk, like Pumpkin and Coconut Soup.

Without doubt the most famous soup is Tom Yam Goong – Hot and Sour Shrimp Soup – a symphony of flavor, it uses many local favorites such as lemongrass, galangal, cilantro, kaffir lime leaves and, of course, chilies.

Pork and Pickled Mustard Greens Soup

INGREDIENTS

Serves 4–6

8 ounces pickled mustard
  greens, soaked
2 ounces cellophane noodles, soaked
1 tablespoon vegetable oil
4 garlic cloves, finely sliced
4 cups chicken stock
1 pound pork ribs, cut into
  large chunks
2 tablespoons fish sauce
pinch of sugar
freshly ground black pepper
2 red chilies, seeded and finely sliced,
  to garnish

3 Heat the oil in a small frying pan, add the garlic and stir-fry until golden. Transfer the mixture to a bowl and set aside.

4 Put the stock in a saucepan, bring to a boil, then add the pork and simmer gently for 10–15 minutes.

5 Add the pickled mustard greens and cellophane noodles. Bring back to a boil. Season to taste with fish sauce, sugar and freshly ground black pepper. Serve hot, topped with the fried garlic and red chilies.

1 Cut the pickled mustard greens into bite-size pieces. Taste to check the seasoning. If they are too salty, then soak them for a little bit longer.

2 Drain the cellophane noodles and cut them into short lengths.

Chiang Mai Noodle Soup

A signature dish of the city of Chiang Mai, this delicious noodle soup has Burmese origins and is the Thai equivalent of the Malaysian "Laksa."

INGREDIENTS

Serves 4–6

2½ cups unsweetened coconut milk
2 tablespoons red curry paste
1 teaspoon ground turmeric
1 pound chicken thighs, boned and cut
   into bite-size chunks
2½ cups chicken stock
4 tablespoons fish sauce
1 tablespoon dark soy sauce
juice of ½–1 lime
1 pound fresh egg noodles, blanched
   briefly in boiling water
salt and freshly ground black pepper

For the garnish

3 scallions, chopped
4 red chilies, chopped
4 shallots, chopped
4 tablespoons sliced pickled mustard
   greens, rinsed
2 tablespoons fried sliced garlic
cilantro leaves
4 fried noodle nests (optional)

1 In a large saucepan, add about one-third of the coconut milk and bring to a boil, stirring often with a wooden spoon until it separates.

2 Add the curry paste and ground turmeric, stir to mix completely and cook until fragrant.

3 Add the chicken and stir-fry for about 2 minutes, ensuring that all the chunks are coated with the paste.

4 Add the remaining coconut milk, chicken stock, fish sauce and soy sauce. Season with salt and freshly ground black pepper to taste. Simmer gently for 7–10 minutes. Remove from the heat and stir in the lime juice.

5 Reheat the noodles in boiling water, drain and divide between individual bowls. Divide the chicken between the bowls and ladle in the hot soup. Top each serving with a few of each of the garnishes.

Ginger, Chicken and Coconut Soup

This aromatic soup is rich with coconut milk and intensely flavored with galangal, lemongrass and kaffir lime leaves.

INGREDIENTS

Serves 4–6

3 cups unsweetened coconut milk
2 cups chicken stock
4 lemongrass stalks, bruised
  and chopped
1-inch piece galangal, thinly sliced
10 black peppercorns, crushed
10 kaffir lime leaves, torn
11 ounces boneless chicken, cut
  into thin strips
1½ cups button mushrooms
5 tablespoons canned baby corn
4 tablespoons lime juice
3 tablespoons fish sauce
2 red chilies, chopped, to garnish
chopped scallions, to garnish
cilantro leaves, to garnish

1 Bring the coconut milk and chicken stock to a boil. Add the lemongrass, galangal, peppercorns and half the kaffir lime leaves, reduce the heat and simmer gently for 10 minutes.

2 Strain the stock into a clean pan. Return to the heat, then add the chicken, button mushrooms and baby corn. Cook for about 5–7 minutes or until the chicken is cooked.

3 Stir in the lime juice, fish sauce to taste and the rest of the lime leaves. Serve hot, garnished with red chilies, scallions and cilantro.

Hot and Sour Shrimp Soup with Lemongrass

This classic Thai seafood soup – *Tom Yam Goong* – is probably the most popular and well-known soup from Thailand.

INGREDIENTS

Serves 4–6

1 pound jumbo shrimp
4 cups chicken stock or water
3 lemongrass stalks
10 kaffir lime leaves, torn in half
8-ounce can straw mushrooms, drained
3 tablespoons fish sauce
¼ cup lime juice
2 tablespoons chopped scallion
1 tablespoon cilantro leaves
4 red chilies, seeded and chopped
2 scallions, finely chopped

1 Shell and devein the shrimp and set aside. Rinse the shrimp shells and place in a large saucepan with the stock or water and bring to a boil.

2 Bruise the lemongrass stalks with the blunt edge of a chopping knife and add them to the stock, together with half the lime leaves. Simmer gently for 5–6 minutes, until the stalks change color and the stock is fragrant.

3 Strain the stock and return to the saucepan and reheat. Add the mushrooms and shrimp, then cook until the shrimp turn pink.

4 Stir in the fish sauce, lime juice, scallions, cilantro, red chilies and the rest of the lime leaves. Taste and adjust the seasoning. It should be sour, salty, spicy and hot.

Pumpkin and Coconut Soup

INGREDIENTS

Serves 4–6

2 garlic cloves, crushed
4 shallots, finely chopped
½ teaspoon shrimp paste
1 tablespoon dried shrimp, soaked for
   10 minutes and drained
1 lemongrass stalk, chopped
2 green chilies, seeded
2½ cups chicken stock
1 pound pumpkin, cut into ¾-inch
   thick chunks
2½ cups coconut cream
2 tablespoons fish sauce
1 teaspoon sugar
4 ounces small cooked
   shelled shrimp
salt and freshly ground black pepper
2 red chilies, seeded and finely
   sliced, and 10–12 basil leaves,
   to garnish

1 Grind the garlic, shallots, shrimp
paste, dried shrimp, lemongrass,
green chilies and salt into a paste.

2 In a large saucepan, bring the
chicken stock to a boil, add the
ground paste and stir to dissolve.

3 Add the pumpkin and simmer for
about 10–15 minutes, or until the
pumpkin is tender.

4 Stir in the coconut cream, then
bring back to a simmer. Add the
fish sauce, sugar and ground black
pepper to taste.

5 Add the shrimp and cook until
they are heated through. Serve
garnished with the sliced red chilies
and basil leaves.

COOK'S TIP

Shrimp paste is used here to give a
wonderful savory flavor.

Spinach and Tofu Soup

An extremely delicate and mild-flavored soup that can be used to counterbalance the heat from a hot Thai curry.

INGREDIENTS

Serves 4–6

2 tablespoons dried shrimp
4 cups chicken stock
8 ounces fresh tofu, drained and cut into ¾-inch cubes
2 tablespoons fish sauce
12 ounces fresh spinach, washed thoroughly
freshly ground black pepper
2 scallions, finely sliced, to garnish

1 Rinse and drain the dried shrimp. Combine the shrimp with the chicken stock in a large saucepan and bring to a boil.

2 Add the tofu and simmer for about 5 minutes. Season with fish sauce and black pepper to taste.

3 Tear the spinach leaves into bite-size pieces and add to the soup. Cook for another 1–2 minutes.

4 Remove from the heat and sprinkle over the finely sliced scallions, to garnish.

COOK'S TIP

Homemade chicken stock makes the world of difference to clear soups. Whenever you have accumulated enough bones, make a big batch of stock, use what you need and keep the rest in the freezer.

Put 3–3½ pounds meaty chicken bones and 1 pound pork bones (optional) into a large saucepan. Add 12 cups water and slowly bring to a boil. Occasionally skim off and discard any scum that rises to the surface. Add 2 slices fresh ginger, 2 garlic cloves (optional), 2 celery stalks, 4 scallions, 2 bruised lemongrass stalks, a few cilantro stalks and 10 crushed black peppercorns. Reduce the heat to low and simmer for about 2–2½ hours. Remove from the heat and let cool, uncovered and undisturbed. Pour through a fine strainer, leaving the last dregs behind as they tend to cloud the soup. Use as required, removing any fat that congeals on the surface.

Salads
and
Vegetables

Thai salads are in a class of their own. In preparing a
salad, a Thai cook will always strive for a mix of
colors, contrasting flavors of hot, sweet, sour and salty,
all combined in perfect harmony. Freshly picked
vegetables, aromatic herbs and flavorful leaves are
chopped, sliced, spiced and blended, then topped with
an array of roasted peanuts, crisp-fried shallots, garlic
and fresh chilies. When slices of meat and seafood are
included, these salads may well be served as a main
course. Use the freshest of ingredients and taste the
food as you assemble the dish. You may find some
things are too sweet, too sour or too salty for your
palate, so adjust the ingredients to suit your taste.
Vegetables may be stir-fried, steamed or boiled, but
keep the cooking time to a minimum in order to retain
all the flavor and goodness.

Eggplant Salad with Dried Shrimp and Egg

An appetizing and unusual salad that you will find yourself making over and over again.

INGREDIENTS

Serves 4–6

2 eggplant
1 tablespoon oil
2 tablespoons dried shrimp, soaked
　and drained
1 tablespoon coarsely chopped garlic
2 tablespoons fresh lime juice
1 teaspoon palm sugar
2 tablespoons fish sauce
1 hard-cooked egg, shelled and
　chopped
4 shallots, finely sliced into rings
cilantro leaves, to garnish
2 red chilies, seeded and sliced,
　to garnish

─────── COOK'S TIP ───────

For an interesting variation, try using salted duck or quail eggs, cut in halves.

1 Broil or roast the eggplant until charred and tender.

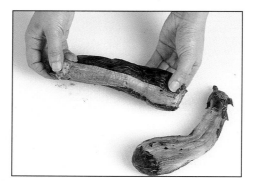

2 When cool enough to handle, peel away the skin and slice the flesh.

3 Heat the oil in a small frying pan, add the drained shrimp and garlic and fry until golden. Remove from the pan and set aside.

4 To make the dressing, put the lime juice, palm sugar and fish sauce in a small bowl and whisk together.

5 To serve, arrange the eggplant on a serving dish. Top with the egg, shallots and dried shrimp mixture. Drizzle over the dressing and garnish with cilantro and red chilies.

Thai Beef Salad

A hearty salad of beef, laced with a chili and lime dressing.

INGREDIENTS

Serves 4

2 x 8-ounce sirloin steaks
1 red onion, finely sliced
½ cucumber, finely sliced into
    matchsticks
1 lemongrass stalk, finely chopped
juice of 2 limes
1–2 tablespoons fish sauce
2 tablespoons chopped scallions
2–4 red chilies, finely sliced, to garnish
fresh cilantro, Chinese mustard cress
    and mint leaves, to garnish

1 Pan-fry or broil the beef steaks to medium-rare. Allow to rest for 10–15 minutes.

2 When cool, thinly slice the beef and put the slices in a large bowl.

3 Add the sliced onion, cucumber matchsticks and lemongrass.

4 Add the scallions. Toss and season with lime juice and fish sauce. Serve at room temperature or chilled, garnished with the chilies, cilantro, Chinese mustard cress and mint.

Larp of Chiang Mai

The city of Chiang Mai in the north-east of Thailand is culturally very close to Laos and famous for its chicken salad, which was originally called "Laap" or "Larp." Duck, beef or pork can be used instead of chicken.

INGREDIENTS

Serves 4–6

1 pound ground chicken
1 lemongrass stalk, finely chopped
3 kaffir lime leaves, finely chopped
4 red chilies, seeded and chopped
4 tablespoons lime juice
2 tablespoons fish sauce
1 tablespoon roasted ground rice
2 scallions, chopped
2 tablespoons cilantro leaves
mixed salad leaves, cucumber and
    tomato slices, to serve
a few sprigs of mint, to garnish

1 Heat a large non-stick frying pan. Add the ground chicken and cook in a little water.

COOK'S TIP

Use sticky, or glutinous, rice to make roasted ground rice. Firstly put the rice in a frying pan and dry-roast it until golden brown. Remove and grind it to a powder in a mortar and pestle or in a food processor. Keep in a glass jar in a cool and dry place and use as required.

2 Stir constantly for about 7–10 minutes until cooked.

3 Transfer the cooked chicken to a large bowl and add the rest of the ingredients. Mix thoroughly.

4 Serve on a bed of mixed salad leaves, cucumber and tomato slices and garnish with sprigs of mint.

Tangy Chicken Salad

This fresh and lively dish typifies the character of Thai cuisine. It is ideal for a snack or light lunch.

INGREDIENTS

Serves 4–6

4 skinned, boneless chicken breasts
2 garlic cloves, crushed and
    coarsely chopped
2 tablespoons soy sauce
2 tablespoons vegetable oil
½ cup coconut cream
2 tablespoons fish sauce
juice of 1 lime
2 tablespoons palm sugar
4 ounces water chestnuts, sliced
½ cup cashews, roasted
4 shallots, finely sliced
4 kaffir lime leaves, finely sliced
1 lemongrass stalk, finely sliced
1 teaspoon chopped galangal
1 large red chili, seeded and
    finely sliced
2 scallions, finely sliced
10–12 mint leaves, torn
1 head of lettuce, to serve
sprigs of cilantro and 2 green or red
    chilies, seeded and sliced, to garnish

1 Trim the chicken breasts of any excess fat and put them in a large dish. Rub with the garlic, soy sauce and 1 tablespoon of the oil. Allow to marinate for 1–2 hours.

2 Broil or pan-fry the chicken for 3–4 minutes on both sides or until cooked. Remove and set aside to cool.

3 In a small saucepan, heat the coconut cream, fish sauce, lime juice and palm sugar. Stir until all of the sugar has dissolved and then remove from the heat.

4 Cut the cooked chicken into strips and combine with the water chestnuts, cashews, shallots, kaffir lime leaves, lemongrass, galangal, red chili, scallions and mint leaves.

5 Pour the coconut dressing over the chicken, toss and mix well. Serve the chicken on a bed of lettuce leaves and garnish with sprigs of cilantro and sliced chilies.

Seafood Salad with Fragrant Herbs

INGREDIENTS

Serves 4–6

1 cup fish stock or water
12 ounces squid, cut into rings
12 uncooked jumbo shrimp, shelled
12 scallops
2 ounces bean thread noodles, soaked
  in warm water for 30 minutes
½ cucumber, cut into thin sticks
1 lemongrass stalk, finely chopped
2 kaffir lime leaves, finely shredded
2 shallots, finely sliced
juice of 1–2 limes
2 tablespoons fish sauce
2 tablespoons chopped scallions
2 tablespoons cilantro leaves
12–15 mint leaves, coarsely torn
4 red chilies, sliced
sprigs of cilantro, to garnish

1 Pour the stock or water into a medium-size saucepan, set over high heat and bring to a boil.

2 Cook each type of seafood separately in the stock for a few minutes. Remove and set aside.

3 Drain the bean thread noodles and cut them into short lengths, about 2 inches long. Combine the noodles with the cooked seafood.

4 Add all the remaining ingredients, mix together well and serve garnished with the cilantro sprigs.

Pomelo Salad

Pomelo is a large fruit that resembles a grapefruit. It has a much sturdier and drier flesh.

INGREDIENTS

Serves 4–6
For the dressing
2 tablespoons fish sauce
1 tablespoon palm sugar
2 tablespoons lime juice

For the salad
2 tablespoons vegetable oil
4 shallots, finely sliced
2 garlic cloves, finely sliced
1 large pomelo
4 ounces cooked, shelled shrimp
4 ounces cooked crab meat
1 tablespoon roasted peanuts
10–12 small mint leaves, chopped
2 scallions, finely sliced, 2 red chilies,
  seeded and finely sliced, cilantro
  leaves and shredded fresh coconut
  (optional), to garnish

1 Whisk together the fish sauce, palm sugar and lime juice and set aside.

2 Heat the oil in a small frying pan, add the shallots and garlic and fry until they are golden. Remove from the pan and set aside.

3 Peel the pomelo and break the flesh into small pieces, taking care to remove any membranes.

4 Coarsely grind the peanuts, then combine with the pomelo flesh, shrimp, crab meat, mint leaves and the fried shallot mixture. Toss in the dressing and serve sprinkled with the scallions, red chilies, cilantro leaves and shredded coconut, if using.

Cabbage Salad

A simple and delicious way of using cabbage. Other vegetables such as broccoli, cauliflower, beansprouts and Chinese cabbage can also be prepared this way.

INGREDIENTS

Serves 4–6

2 tablespoons fish sauce
grated rind of 1 lime
2 tablespoons lime juice
½ cup unsweetened coconut milk
2 tablespoons vegetable oil
2 large red chilies, seeded and finely cut
    into strips
6 garlic cloves, finely sliced
6 shallots, finely sliced
1 small cabbage, shredded
2 tablespoons coarsely chopped roasted
    peanuts, to serve

1 Make the dressing by combining the fish sauce, lime rind and juice and coconut milk. Set aside.

2 Heat the oil in a wok or frying pan. Stir-fry the chilies, garlic and shallots, until the shallots are brown and crisp. Remove and set aside.

3 Blanch the cabbage in boiling salted water for about 2–3 minutes, drain and put into a bowl.

4 Stir the dressing into the cabbage, toss and mix well. Transfer the salad to a serving dish. Sprinkle with the fried shallot mixture and the chopped roasted peanuts.

Bamboo Shoot Salad

This salad, which has a hot and sharp flavor, originated in northeast Thailand. Use fresh young bamboo shoots when you can find them, otherwise substitute canned bamboo shoots.

INGREDIENTS

Serves 4

14-ounce can whole bamboo shoots
1 ounce glutinous (sticky) rice
2 tablespoons chopped shallots
1 tablespoon chopped garlic
3 tablespoons chopped scallions
2 tablespoons fish sauce
2 tablespoons lime juice
1 teaspoon sugar
½ teaspoon dried flaked chilies
20–25 small mint leaves
1 tablespoon toasted sesame seeds

3 Turn the rice into a bowl, add the shallots, garlic, scallions, fish sauce, lime juice, sugar, chilies and half the mint leaves.

4 Mix thoroughly, then pour over the bamboo shoots and toss together. Serve sprinkled with sesame seeds and the remaining mint leaves.

1 Rinse and drain the bamboo shoots, finely slice and set aside.

2 Dry-roast the rice in a frying pan until it is golden brown. Remove and grind to fine crumbs with a mortar and pestle.

Stir-fried Bean Sprouts

Sprouted from mung beans, bean sprouts have a delicate taste, they are very nutritious and also easy to digest. They are widely available in most supermarkets.

INGREDIENTS

Serves 4–6

2 tablespoons oil
2 garlic cloves, chopped
1 tablespoon dried shrimp, soaked and rinsed
4 ounces ground lean pork
1 cup bean sprouts
4 ounces garlic chives, chopped
1 tablespoon fish sauce
1 teaspoon superfine sugar
freshly ground black pepper
cilantro leaves, to garnish

1 Heat the oil in a wok or deep frying pan. Add the garlic and dried shrimp and fry until golden.

2 Add the pork and fry over high heat for 3–5 minutes, or until the pork is cooked.

3 Add the bean sprouts, garlic chives, fish sauce, sugar and pepper. Serve garnished with cilantro leaves.

— COOK'S TIP —

If you like, you can use ground chicken or beef instead of pork. For a vegetarian version, substitute fried tofu.

Green Papaya Salad

There are many variations of this salad in South-East Asia. As green papaya is not easy to get hold of, shredded carrots, cucumber or green apple may also be used. Serve this salad with raw Chinese or white cabbage and rice.

INGREDIENTS

Serves 4

1 medium-size green papaya
4 garlic cloves
1 tablespoon chopped shallot
3–4 red chilies, seeded and sliced
$\frac{1}{2}$ teaspoon salt
2–3 snake beans (or green or runner beans), cut into $\frac{3}{4}$-inch lengths
2 tomatoes, cut into wedges
3 tablespoons fish sauce
1 tablespoon superfine sugar
juice of 1 lime
2 tablespoons crushed roasted peanuts
sliced red chilies, to garnish

1 Peel the papaya and cut in half lengthwise, scrape out the seeds with a spoon and finely shred the flesh.

— COOK'S TIP —

If you do not have a large mortar and pestle, use a bowl and crush the shredded papaya with a wooden meat tenderizer or the end of a rolling pin.

2 Grind the garlic, shallots, chilies and salt together in a large mortar with a pestle.

3 Add the shredded papaya a little at a time and pound until it becomes slightly limp and soft.

4 Add the sliced beans and tomatoes and lightly crush. Season with fish sauce, sugar and lime juice.

5 Transfer the salad to a serving dish, sprinkle with crushed peanuts and garnish with the red chilies.

Water Spinach with Brown Bean Sauce

Water spinach, often known as Siamese watercress, is a green vegetable with arrowhead–shaped leaves. If you can't find it, use spinach, watercress, *bok choy* or even broccoli, and adjust the cooking time accordingly. There are excellent variations to this recipe using black bean sauce, instead of brown bean sauce.

INGREDIENTS

Serves 4–6
1 bunch water spinach, about
   2¼ pounds in weight
3 tablespoons vegetable oil
1 tablespoon chopped garlic
1 tablespoon brown bean sauce
2 tablespoons fish sauce
1 tablespoon sugar
freshly ground black pepper

1 Trim and discard the bottom coarse, woody end of the water spinach. Cut the remaining part into 2-inch lengths, keeping the leaves separate from the stems.

2 Heat the oil in a wok or large frying pan. When it starts to smoke, add the chopped garlic and toss for 10 seconds.

3 Add the stem part of the water spinach, let it sizzle and cook for 1 minute, then add the leafy parts.

4 Stir in the brown bean sauce, fish sauce, sugar and pepper. Toss and turn over the spinach until it begins to wilt, about 3–4 minutes. Transfer to a serving dish and serve immediately.

Mixed Vegetables in Coconut Milk

A most delicious way of cooking vegetables. If you don't like highly spiced food, use fewer red chili peppers.

INGREDIENTS

Serves 4–6
1 pound mixed vegetables, such as
   eggplant, baby canned corn, carrots,
   snake beans and patty pan squash
8 red chilies, seeded
2 lemongrass stalks, chopped
4 kaffir lime leaves, torn
2 tablespoons vegetable oil
1 cup unsweetened coconut milk
2 tablespoons fish sauce
a pinch of salt
15–20 Thai basil leaves, to garnish

1 Cut the vegetables into similar size shapes using a sharp knife.

2 Put the red chilies, lemongrass and kaffir lime leaves in a mortar and grind together with a pestle.

3 Heat the oil in a wok or large deep frying pan. Add the chili mixture and fry for 2–3 minutes.

4 Stir in the coconut milk and bring to a boil. Add the vegetables and cook for about 5 minutes, or until they are tender. Season with the fish sauce and salt, and garnish with basil leaves.

Main Courses

Thailand has a tropical cornucopia of good things to eat
and its coastal regions yield an abundance of seafood,
both tempting and exotic.

Thais do not divide meals into courses as Westerners
do; instead all the dishes are brought out and served at
once. A typical meal is a compilation of four to five
different dishes with contrasting textures and flavors.
These dishes will nearly always include a clear soup,
different meats, fried or steamed seafood and vegetable
dishes, a curry, a salad, one or two hot sauces
and, of course, rice.

There should be no duplication or repetition, and
ingredients and colors should be as diverse as possible.
This reflects the influence of the Chinese principle of
yin and yang; the idea is to achieve overall healthful
harmony by balancing opposing qualities.

Shrimp Satay

Serve this enticing and tasty dish with greens and jasmine rice.

INGREDIENTS

Serves 4–6
1 pound jumbo shrimp, shelled, tail ends left intact and deveined
½ bunch cilantro leaves, to garnish
4 red chilies, finely sliced and scallions, cut diagonally, to garnish

For the peanut sauce

3 tablespoons vegetable oil
1 tablespoon chopped garlic
1 small onion, chopped
3–4 red chilies, crushed and chopped
3 kaffir lime leaves, torn
1 lemongrass stalk, bruised and chopped
1 teaspoon medium curry paste
1 cup unsweetened coconut milk
½-inch cinnamon stick
⅓ cup crunchy peanut butter
3 tablespoons tamarind juice
2 tablespoons fish sauce
2 tablespoons palm sugar
juice of ½ lemon

1 To make the sauce, heat half the oil in a wok or large frying pan and add the garlic and onion. Cook for about 3–4 minutes, until it softens.

2 Add the chilies, kaffir lime leaves, lemongrass and curry paste. Cook for a further 2–3 minutes.

COOK'S TIP

Curry paste has a far superior, authentic flavor to powdered varieties. Once opened, it should be kept in the fridge and used within two months.

3 Stir in the coconut milk, cinnamon stick, peanut butter, tamarind juice, fish sauce, palm sugar and lemon juice.

4 Reduce the heat and simmer gently for 15–20 minutes until the sauce thickens, stirring occasionally to make sure that the sauce doesn't stick to the bottom of the pan.

5 Heat the rest of the oil in a wok or large frying pan. Add the shrimp and stir-fry for about 3–4 minutes, or until the shrimp turn pink and are slightly firm to the touch.

6 Mix the shrimp with the sauce. Serve garnished with cilantro leaves, red chilies and scallions.

Sweet and Sour Fish

When fish is cooked in this way the skin becomes crispy on the outside, while the flesh remains moist and juicy inside. The sweet and sour sauce, with its colorful cherry tomatoes, complements the fish beautifully.

INGREDIENTS

Serves 4–6

1 large or 2 medium-size fish such as snapper or mullet, heads removed
2 tablespoons cornstarch
1/2 cup vegetable oil
1 tablespoon chopped garlic
1 tablespoon chopped fresh ginger
2 tablespoons chopped shallots
8 ounces cherry tomatoes
2 tablespoons red wine vinegar
2 tablespoons sugar
2 tablespoons tomato ketchup
1 tablespoon fish sauce
3 tablespoons water
salt and freshly ground black pepper
cilantro leaves and shredded scallions, to garnish

1 Thoroughly rinse and clean the fish. Score the skin diagonally on both sides of the fish.

2 Coat the fish lightly on both sides with 1 tablespoon cornstarch. Shake off any excess.

3 Heat the oil in a wok or large frying pan and slide the fish into the wok. Reduce the heat to medium and fry the fish for about 6–7 minutes, until crisp and brown on both sides.

4 Remove the fish with a spatula and place on a large platter.

5 Pour off all but 2 tablespoons of the oil and add the garlic, ginger and shallots. Fry until golden.

6 Add the cherry tomatoes and cook until they burst open. Stir in the vinegar, sugar, tomato ketchup and fish sauce. Simmer gently for 1–2 minutes and adjust the seasoning to taste.

7 Blend the remaining 1 tablespoon cornstarch with the water. Stir into the sauce and heat until it thickens. Pour the sauce over the fish and garnish with cilantro leaves and shredded scallions.

Baked Fish in Banana Leaves

Fish that is prepared in this way is particularly succulent and flavorful. Fillets are used here rather than whole fish – easier for those who don't like to mess around with bones. It is a great dish for outdoor barbecues.

INGREDIENTS

Serves 4

1 cup unsweetened coconut milk
2 tablespoons red curry paste
3 tablespoons fish sauce
2 tablespoons superfine sugar
5 kaffir lime leaves, torn
4 x 6-ounce fish fillets, such as snapper
6 ounces mixed vegetables, such as carrots or leeks, finely shredded
4 banana leaves, or aluminum foil
2 tablespoons shredded scallions and 2 red chilies, finely sliced, to garnish

1 Combine the coconut milk, curry paste, fish sauce, sugar and kaffir lime leaves in a shallow dish.

2 Marinate the fish in this mixture for about 15–30 minutes. Preheat the oven to 400°F.

3 Mix the vegetables together and lay a portion on top of a banana leaf or piece of foil. Place a piece of fish on top with a little of its marinade.

4 Wrap the fish up by turning in the sides and ends of the leaf and secure with toothpicks. Repeat with the rest of the leaves and the fish.

5 Bake in the hot oven for 20–25 minutes or until the fish is cooked. Alternatively, cook under the broiler or on the barbecue. Just before serving, garnish the fish with a sprinkling of scallions and sliced red chilies.

Stir-fried Scallops with Asparagus

Asparagus is extremely popular among the Chinese Thai. The combination of garlic and black pepper gives this dish its spiciness. You can substitute the scallops with shrimp or other firm fish.

INGREDIENTS

Serves 4–6

4 tablespoons vegetable oil
1 bunch asparagus, cut into 2-inch lengths
4 garlic cloves, finely chopped
2 shallots, finely chopped
1 pound scallops, cleaned
2 tablespoons fish sauce
½ teaspoon coarsely ground black pepper
½ cup unsweetened coconut milk
cilantro leaves, to garnish

1 Heat half the oil in a wok or large frying pan. Add the asparagus and stir-fry for about 2 minutes. Transfer the asparagus to a plate and set aside.

2 Add the rest of the oil, garlic and shallots to the same wok and fry until fragrant. Add the scallops and cook for another 1–2 minutes.

3 Return the asparagus to the wok. Add the fish sauce, black pepper and coconut milk.

4 Stir and cook for about another 3–4 minutes or until the scallops and asparagus are cooked. Garnish with the cilantro leaves.

Steamed Fish with Chili Sauce

Steaming is one of the best methods of cooking fish. By leaving the fish whole and on the bone, you'll find that all the flavor and moistness is retained.

INGREDIENTS

Serves 4

1 large or 2 medium firm fish, such as bass or grouper, scaled and cleaned
1 banana leaf or aluminum foil
2 tablespoons rice wine
3 red chilies, seeded and finely sliced
2 garlic cloves, finely chopped
3/4-inch piece fresh ginger, finely shredded
2 lemongrass stalks, crushed and finely chopped
2 scallions, chopped
2 tablespoons fish sauce
juice of 1 lime

For the chili sauce

10 red chilies, seeded and chopped
4 garlic cloves, chopped
4 tablespoons fish sauce
1 tablespoon sugar
5 tablespoons lime juice

1 Rinse the fish under cold running water. Pat dry with paper towels. With a sharp knife, slash the skin of the fish a few times on both sides.

2 Place the fish on a banana leaf or piece of foil. Mix all the other ingredients and spread over the fish.

3 Place a small upturned plate or rack in the bottom of a wok and add about 2 inches boiling water. Lift the banana leaf, together with the fish, and place on the plate or rack. Cover with a lid and steam for about 10–15 minutes, or until the fish is cooked.

4 Place all the chili sauce ingredients in a food processor and process until smooth. You may need to add a little cold water.

5 Serve the fish hot, on the banana leaf if you like, with the sweet chili sauce to spoon over the top.

Stir-fried Shrimp with Tamarind

The sour, tangy flavor that is characteristic of many Thai dishes comes from tamarind. Fresh tamarind pods, from the tamarind tree, can sometimes be bought, but preparing them for cooking is a laborious process. The Thais prefer to use compressed blocks of tamarind paste, which is simply soaked in warm water and then strained.

INGREDIENTS

Serves 4–6

2 tablespoons tamarind paste
⅔ cup boiling water
2 tablespoons vegetable oil
2 tablespoons chopped onion
2 tablespoons palm sugar
2 tablespoons chicken stock or water
1 tablespoon fish sauce
6 dried red chilies, fried
1 pound uncooked shelled shrimp
1 tablespoon fried chopped garlic
2 tablespoons fried sliced shallots
2 scallions, chopped, to garnish

1 Put the tamarind paste in a small bowl, pour over the boiling water and stir well to break up any lumps. Set aside for 30 minutes. Strain, pushing as much of the juice through as possible. Measure 6 tablespoons of the juice, which is the amount needed, and store the rest in the fridge. Heat the oil in a wok. Add the chopped onion and fry until golden brown.

2 Add the sugar, stock, fish sauce, dried chilies and the tamarind juice, stirring well until the sugar dissolves. Bring to a boil.

3 Add the shrimp, garlic and shallots. Stir-fry for about 3–4 minutes until the shrimp are cooked. Garnish with the chopped scallions.

Chicken Livers, Thai-style

Chicken liver is a good source of iron and is a popular meat, especially in the north-east. Serve this dish as an appetizer with salad, or as part of a main course with jasmine rice.

INGREDIENTS

Serves 4–6

3 tablespoons vegetable oil
1 pound chicken livers, trimmed
4 shallots, chopped
2 garlic cloves, chopped
1 tablespoon roasted ground rice
3 tablespoons fish sauce
3 tablespoons lime juice
1 teaspoon sugar
2 lemongrass stalks, bruised
  and finely chopped
2 tablespoons chopped cilantro
10–12 mint leaves, to garnish

1 Heat the oil in a wok or large frying pan. Add the livers and fry over medium-high heat for about 4 minutes, until the liver is golden brown and cooked, but still pink inside.

2 Move the liver to one side of the pan and add the shallots and garlic. Fry for about 1–2 minutes.

3 Add the roasted ground rice, fish sauce, lime juice, sugar, lemongrass and cilantro. Stir to combine. Remove from the heat and serve garnished with mint leaves.

Barbecued Chicken

Barbecued chicken is served almost everywhere in Thailand, from roadside stalls to sports stadiums and beaches.

INGREDIENTS

Serves 4–6

1 chicken, about 3–3½ pounds, cut
  into 8–10 pieces
2 limes, cut into wedges and 2 red
  chilies, finely sliced, to garnish

For the marinade

2 lemongrass stalks, chopped
1-inch piece fresh ginger
6 garlic cloves
4 shallots
½ bunch cilantro roots
1 tablespoon palm sugar
½ cup unsweetened coconut milk
2 tablespoons fish sauce
2 tablespoons soy sauce

1 To make the marinade, put all the ingredients into a food processor and process until smooth.

2 Put the chicken pieces in a dish and pour over the marinade. Set aside in a cool place to marinate for at least 4 hours or overnight.

3 Barbecue the chicken over glowing coals, or place on a rack over a baking pan and bake at 400°F for about 20–30 minutes, or until the chicken is cooked and golden brown. Turn the pieces occasionally and brush them with the marinade.

4 Garnish with lime wedges and finely sliced red chilies.

Cashew Chicken

In this Chinese-inspired dish, tender pieces of chicken are stir-fried with cashew nuts, red chillies and a touch of garlic, for a delicious combination.

INGREDIENTS

Serves 4–6

450g/1lb boneless chicken breasts
30ml/2 tbsp vegetable oil
2 garlic cloves, sliced
4 dried red chillies, chopped
1 red pepper, seeded and cut into
  2cm/³⁄₄in dice
30ml/2 tbsp oyster sauce
15ml/1 tbsp soy sauce
pinch of granulated sugar
1 bunch spring onions, cut into
  5cm/2in lengths
175g/6oz cashew nuts, roasted
coriander leaves, to garnish

1 Remove and discard the skin from the chicken breasts. With a sharp knife, cut the chicken into bite-size pieces and set aside.

2 Heat the oil in a wok and swirl it around. Add the garlic and dried chillies and fry until golden.

3 Add the chicken and stir-fry until it changes colour, then add the red pepper. If necessary, add a little water.

4 Stir in the oyster sauce, soy sauce and sugar. Add the spring onions and cashew nuts. Stir-fry for about another 1–2 minutes. Serve garnished with coriander leaves.

Stir-fried Chicken with Basil and Chilies

This quick and easy chicken dish is an excellent introduction to Thai cuisine. Deep-frying the basil adds another dimension to this dish. Thai basil, which is sometimes known as Holy basil, has a unique, pungent flavor that is both spicy and sharp. The dull leaves have serrated edges.

INGREDIENTS

Serves 4–6

3 tablespoons vegetable oil
4 garlic cloves, sliced
2–4 red chilies, seeded
  and chopped
1 pound chicken, cut into
  bite-size pieces
2–3 tablespoons fish sauce
2 teaspoons dark soy sauce
1 teaspoon sugar
10–12 Thai basil leaves
2 red chilies, finely sliced and 20 Thai
  basil leaves, deep-fried (optional),
  to garnish

1 Heat the oil in a wok or large frying pan and swirl it around.

COOK'S TIP

To deep-fry Thai basil leaves, make sure that the leaves are completely dry. Deep-fry in hot oil for about 30–40 seconds, lift out and drain on paper towels.

2 Add the garlic and chilies and stir-fry until golden.

3 Add the chicken and stir-fry until it changes color.

4 Season with fish sauce, soy sauce and sugar. Continue to stir-fry for 3–4 minutes, or until the chicken is cooked. Stir in the fresh Thai basil leaves. Garnish with sliced chilies and the deep-fried basil, if using.

Fragrant Thai Meatballs

INGREDIENTS

Serves 4–6
1 pound lean ground pork or beef
1 tablespoon chopped garlic
1 lemongrass stalk, finely chopped
4 scallions, finely chopped
1 tablespoon chopped fresh cilantro
2 tablespoons red curry paste
1 tablespoon lemon juice
1 tablespoon fish sauce
1 egg
rice flour for dusting
oil for frying
salt and freshly ground black pepper
sprigs of cilantro, to garnish

For the peanut sauce
1 tablespoon vegetable oil
1 tablespoon red curry paste
2 tablespoons crunchy peanut butter
1 tablespoon palm sugar
1 tablespoon lemon juice
1 cup unsweetened coconut milk

1 To make the peanut sauce, heat the oil in a small saucepan, add the curry paste and fry for 1 minute.

2 Stir in the rest of the ingredients and bring to a boil. Lower the heat and simmer for 5 minutes, until the sauce thickens.

3 To make the meatballs, combine all the ingredients except the rice flour, oil and cilantro, and season. Mix everything together thoroughly.

4 Roll and shape the meat into small balls about the size of a walnut. Dust the meatballs with rice flour.

5 Heat the oil in a wok until hot and deep fry the meatballs in batches until nicely browned and cooked through. Drain on paper towels. Serve garnished with sprigs of cilantro and accompanied by the peanut sauce.

Stuffed Thai Omelet

INGREDIENTS

Serves 4
2 tablespoons vegetable oil
2 garlic cloves, finely chopped
1 small onion, finely chopped
8 ounces ground pork
2 tablespoons fish sauce
1 teaspoon sugar
freshly ground black pepper
2 tomatoes, peeled and chopped
1 tablespoon chopped fresh cilantro

For the omelet
5–6 eggs
1 tablespoon fish sauce
2 tablespoons vegetable oil
sprigs of cilantro and red chilies, sliced, to garnish

1 First heat the oil in a wok or frying pan. Add the garlic and onion and fry for 3–4 minutes, until softened. Stir in the pork and fry for about 7–10 minutes, until lightly browned.

2 Add the fish sauce, sugar, freshly ground pepper and tomatoes. Stir to combine and simmer until the sauce thickens slightly. Mix in the chopped fresh cilantro.

3 To make the omelets, whisk together the eggs and fish sauce.

4 Heat 1 tablespoon of the oil in an omelet pan or wok. Add half the beaten egg and tilt the pan to spread the egg into a thin even sheet.

5 When set, spoon half the filling over the center of the omelet. Fold in opposite sides; first the top and bottom, then the right and left sides to make a neat square package.

6 Slide out on to a warm serving dish, folded-side down. Repeat with the rest of the oil, eggs and filling. Serve garnished with sprigs of cilantro and red chilies.

Sweet and Sour Pork, Thai-style

Sweet and sour is traditionally a Chinese creation, but the Thais do it very well. This version has an altogether fresher and cleaner flavor and it makes a good one-dish meal with rice.

INGREDIENTS

Serves 4

12 ounces lean pork
2 tablespoons vegetable oil
4 garlic cloves, finely sliced
1 small red onion, sliced
2 tablespoons fish sauce
1 tablespoon sugar
1 red bell pepper, seeded and diced
½ cucumber, seeded and sliced
2 plum tomatoes, cut into wedges
4 ounces pineapple, cut into
   small chunks
freshly ground black pepper
2 scallions, cut into short lengths
cilantro leaves and shredded scallions,
   to garnish

1 Slice the pork into thin strips. Heat the oil in a wok or large frying pan.

2 Add the garlic and fry until golden, then add the pork and stir-fry for about 4–5 minutes. Add the onion.

3 Season with fish sauce, sugar and freshly ground black pepper. Stir and cook for 3–4 minutes, or until the pork is cooked.

4 Add the rest of the vegetables, the pineapple and scallions. You may need to add a few tablespoons of water. Continue to stir-fry for about another 3–4 minutes. Serve hot, garnished with cilantro leaves and scallions.

Lemongrass Pork Chops with Portobellos

This is a favorite recipe for a barbecue. The enticing aroma of the sizzling meat on the grill makes it popular with everyone.

INGREDIENTS

Serves 4

4 pork chops
4 large Portobello mushrooms
3 tablespoons vegetable oil
4 red chilies, seeded and finely sliced
3 tablespoons fish sauce
6 tablespoons lime juice
4 shallots, chopped
1 teaspoon roasted ground rice
2 tablespoons scallions, chopped
cilantro leaves and shredded scallions, to garnish

For the marinade

2 garlic cloves, chopped
1 tablespoon sugar
1 tablespoon fish sauce
2 tablespoons soy sauce
1 tablespoon sesame oil
1 tablespoon whiskey or dry sherry
2 lemongrass stalks, finely chopped
2 scallions, chopped

1 To make the marinade, mix together all the marinade ingredients.

2 Pour over the pork chops and let marinate for 1–2 hours.

3 Place the mushrooms and marinated pork chops on a broiler pan and brush with 1 tablespoon of the oil. Broil the pork chops for about 5–7 minutes on each side and the mushrooms for about 2 minutes. Brush both with the marinade while broiling.

4 Meanwhile heat the rest of the oil in a small frying pan, then remove from the heat and mix in the remaining ingredients. Put the pork chops and mushrooms on a serving plate and spoon over the sauce. Garnish with cilantro and shredded scallions.

Savory Pork Ribs with Snake Beans

This is a rich and pungent dish. If snake beans are hard to find, you can substitute fine green beans or wax beans.

INGREDIENTS

Serves 4–6

1½ pounds pork spare ribs or boneless pork loin
2 tablespoons vegetable oil
½ cup water
1 tablespoon palm sugar
1 tablespoon fish sauce
5 ounces snake beans, cut into 2-inch lengths
2 kaffir lime leaves, finely sliced
2 red chilies, finely sliced, to garnish

For the chili paste
3 dried red chilies, seeded and soaked
4 shallots, chopped
4 garlic cloves, chopped
1 teaspoon chopped galangal
1 lemongrass stalk, chopped
6 black peppercorns
1 teaspoon shrimp paste
2 tablespoons dried shrimp, rinsed

1 Put all the ingredients for the chili paste in a mortar and grind together with a pestle until it forms a thick paste.

2 Slice and chop the spare ribs (or pork loin) into 1½-inch lengths.

3 Heat the oil in a wok or frying pan. Add the pork and fry for about 5 minutes, until lightly browned.

4 Stir in the chili paste and continue to cook for another 5 minutes, stirring constantly to keep the paste from sticking to the pan.

5 Add the water, cover and simmer for 7–10 minutes, or until the spare ribs are tender. Season with palm sugar and fish sauce.

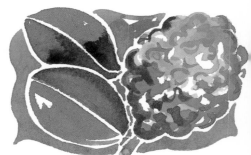

6 Mix in the snake beans and kaffir lime leaves and fry until the beans are cooked. Serve garnished with sliced red chilies.

Stir-fried Beef in Oyster Sauce

Another simple but delicious recipe. In Thailand, fresh straw mushrooms are readily available, but oyster mushrooms make a good substitute. To make the dish even more interesting, use several types of mushroom.

INGREDIENTS

Serves 4–6

1 pound round steak
2 tablespoons soy sauce
1 tablespoon cornstarch
3 tablespoons vegetable oil
1 tablespoon chopped garlic
1 tablespoon chopped fresh ginger
8 ounces mixed mushrooms, such as shiitake, oyster and straw
2 tablespoons oyster sauce
1 teaspoon sugar
4 scallions, cut into short lengths
freshly ground black pepper
2 red chilies, cut into strips, to garnish

1 Slice the beef, on the diagonal, into long thin strips. Mix together the soy sauce and cornstarch in a large bowl, stir in the beef and let marinate for 1–2 hours.

COOK'S TIP

Made from extracts of oysters, oyster sauce is velvety smooth and has a savory sweet and meaty taste. There are several types available; buy the best you can afford.

2 Heat half the oil in a wok or frying pan. Add the garlic and ginger and fry until fragrant. Stir in the beef. Stir to separate the strips, let them color and cook for 1–2 minutes. Remove from the pan and set aside.

3 Heat the remaining oil in the wok. Add the shiitake, oyster and straw mushrooms. Cook until tender.

4 Return the beef to the wok with the mushrooms. Add the oyster sauce, sugar and freshly ground black pepper to taste. Mix well.

5 Add the scallions and mix together well. Serve garnished with strips of red chili.

Steamed Eggs with Beef and Scallions

This is a very delicate dish. You can add less liquid for a firmer custard, but cooked this way it is soft and silky. Other types of meat or seafood can be used instead of the beef.

INGREDIENTS

Serves 4–6

4 ounces sirloin or round steak
1 teaspoon grated fresh ginger
1 tablespoon fish sauce
3 eggs
½ cup chicken stock or water
2 tablespoons finely chopped
   scallions
1 tablespoon vegetable oil
2 garlic cloves, finely sliced
freshly ground black pepper

1 Finely chop the beef and place in a large bowl. Add the ginger, fish sauce and freshly ground black pepper.

2 Beat the eggs together with the stock. Stir the mixture into the beef, add the scallions and beat together until well-blended. Try to avoid making too many bubbles.

3 Pour the mixture into a heatproof dish or individual ramekins.

4 Place in a steamer and steam over gentle heat for 10–15 minutes, or until the custard is set.

5 Meanwhile, heat the oil in a frying pan. Add the garlic, and stir to break up any lumps and fry for about 2 minutes, until golden.

6 To serve, pour the garlic and oil over the egg custards. Allow to cool slightly before serving.

COOK'S TIP

The Japanese make a similar version of this recipe called *Chewan Mushi,* using spinach, shrimp and shiitake mushrooms.

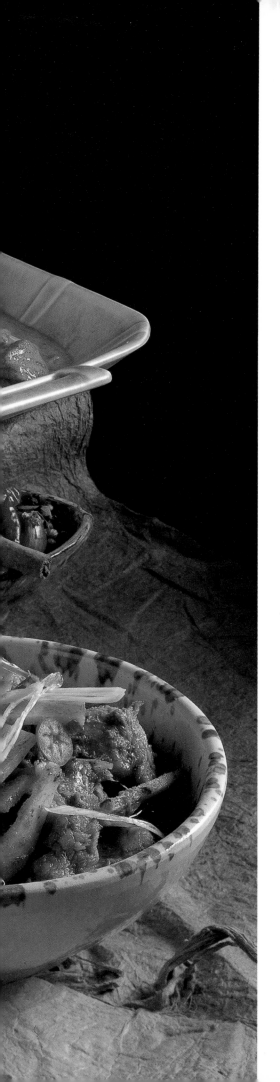

CURRIES

All curry-making begins with the curry paste. In days gone by, each household would have its own recipes, handed down from generation to generation. Various herbs and spices are used, such as lemongrass, kaffir lime leaves, chilies, galangal, cilantro and other flavorings. Everything is crushed with a mortar and pestle, resulting in an aromatic and fragrant wet paste, which can range from mild to extremely hot.

The hottest are the green curry pastes.

Curries originated in southern India, but unlike Indian curries, which use a lot of dried powdered spices and are thick and simmered for many hours, Thai curries are fresher and much lighter. They are usually thin and soup-like and require a lot less cooking, with the exception of Mussaman Curry.

Curries in Thailand are always part of a selection of dishes in a main meal and the heat is usually balanced by a blander or sweeter flavored dish.

Red Chicken Curry with Bamboo Shoots

Bamboo shoots have a lovely crunchy texture. It is quite acceptable to use canned bamboo, as fresh bamboo is not readily available in the West. Whenever you can, buy whole canned bamboo as it is generally crisper and of better quality than sliced shoots. Rinse the bamboo well before using.

INGREDIENTS

Serves 4–6

4 cups unsweetened coconut milk
1 pound diced boneless chicken
2 tablespoons fish sauce
1 tablespoon sugar
8 ounces bamboo shoots, rinsed
  and sliced
5 kaffir lime leaves, torn
salt and freshly ground black pepper
2 red chilies, chopped, 10–12 basil
  leaves and 10–12 mint leaves,
  to garnish

For the red curry paste

12–15 red chilies, seeded
4 shallots, thinly sliced
2 garlic cloves, chopped
1 tablespoon chopped galangal
2 lemongrass stalks, chopped
3 kaffir lime leaves, chopped
4 cilantro roots
10 black peppercorns
1 teaspoon coriander seeds
½ teaspoon cumin seeds
good pinch of ground cinnamon
1 teaspoon ground turmeric
½ teaspoon shrimp paste
1 teaspoon salt
2 tablespoons oil

1 To make the red curry paste, combine all the ingredients in a mortar, except for the oil, and pound with a pestle, or process in a food processor until smooth.

2 Add the oil a little at a time and blend in well. Place in a jar in the fridge until ready to use.

3 In a large heavy-based saucepan, bring half the coconut milk to a boil, stirring until it separates.

4 Add 2 tablespoons of the red curry paste and cook for a few minutes.

5 Add the chicken, fish sauce and sugar. Fry for 3–5 minutes until the chicken changes color, stirring constantly to prevent it from sticking.

6 Add the rest of the coconut milk, bamboo shoots and kaffir lime leaves. Bring back to a boil. Adjust the seasoning to taste. Serve garnished with chilies, basil and mint leaves.

Tofu and Green Bean Red Curry

This is another curry that is simple and quick to make. This recipe uses green beans, but you can use almost any kind of vegetable, such as eggplant, bamboo shoots or broccoli.

INGREDIENTS

Serves 4–6

2½ cups unsweetened coconut milk
1 tablespoon red curry paste
3 tablespoons fish sauce
2 teaspoons palm sugar
3½ cups button mushrooms
4 ounces green beans, trimmed
6 ounces tofu, rinsed and cut into
  ¾-inch cubes
4 kaffir lime leaves, torn
2 red chilies, sliced
cilantro leaves, to garnish

1 Put about one-third of the coconut milk in a wok or saucepan. Cook until it starts to separate and an oily sheen appears.

2 Add the red curry paste, fish sauce and sugar to the coconut milk. Mix together thoroughly.

3 Add the mushrooms. Stir and cook for 1 minute.

4 Stir in the rest of the coconut milk and bring back to a boil.

5 Add the green beans and cubes of tofu and simmer gently for another 4–5 minutes.

6 Stir in the kaffir lime leaves and chilies. Serve garnished with the cilantro leaves.

Burmese-style Pork Curry

Burmese-style curries use pork instead of chicken or beef and water rather than coconut milk. The flavors of this delicious dish improve when it is reheated.

INGREDIENTS

Serves 4–6

1-inch piece fresh ginger, crushed
8 dried red chilies, soaked in warm
 water for 20 minutes
2 lemongrass stalks, finely chopped
1 tablespoon chopped galangal
1 tablespoon shrimp paste
2 tablespoons brown sugar
1 pound pork, with some of its fat
2½ cups water
2 teaspoons ground turmeric
1 teaspoon dark soy sauce
4 shallots, finely chopped
1 tablespoon chopped garlic
3 tablespoons tamarind juice
1 teaspoon sugar
1 tablespoon fish sauce
green beans, to serve
red chilies, to garnish

1 In a mortar, pound the ginger, chilies, lemongrass and galangal into a coarse paste with a pestle, then add the shrimp paste and brown sugar to produce a dark, grainy purée.

2 Cut the pork into large chunks and place in a large heavy-bottomed pan. Add the curry purée and stir to coat the meat thoroughly.

3 Cook over low heat, stirring occasionally, until the meat has changed color and rendered some of its fat and the curry paste is fragrant.

4 Stir in the water, turmeric and soy sauce. Simmer until the meat is tender, for about 40 minutes.

5 Add the shallots, garlic, tamarind juice, sugar and fish sauce. Serve with freshly cooked green beans, and garnish with chilies.

Thick Beef Curry in Sweet Peanut Sauce

This curry is deliciously rich and thicker than most other Thai curries. Serve it with boiled jasmine rice and salted duck's eggs, if you like.

INGREDIENTS

Serves 4–6
2½ cups unsweetened coconut milk
3 tablespoons red curry paste
3 tablespoons fish sauce
2 tablespoons palm sugar
2 lemongrass stalks, bruised
1 pound round steak cut into
   thin strips
¾ cup roasted ground peanuts
2 red chilies, sliced
5 kaffir lime leaves, torn
salt and freshly ground black pepper
2 salted eggs, to serve
10–15 Thai basil leaves, to garnish

1 Put half the coconut milk into a heavy-bottomed saucepan and heat, stirring, until it boils and separates.

───── COOK'S TIP ─────

If you don't have the time to make your own red curry paste, you can buy a ready-made Thai curry paste. There is a wide range available in most supermarkets.

2 Add the red curry paste and cook until fragrant. Add the fish sauce, palm sugar and lemongrass.

3 Continue to cook until the color deepens. Add the rest of the coconut milk. Bring back to a boil.

4 Add the beef and ground peanuts. Stir and cook for 8–10 minutes or until most of the liquid has evaporated.

5 Add the chilies and kaffir lime leaves. Adjust the seasoning to taste. Serve with salted eggs and garnish with Thai basil leaves.

Mussaman Curry

Traditionally this sweet and spicy curry is made with beef, but chicken or lamb can be used instead. You can also make a vegetarian version using tofu.

INGREDIENTS

Serves 4–6
2½ cups unsweetened coconut milk
1½ pounds stewing beef, cut into
   1-inch chunks
1 cup coconut cream
3 tablespoons Mussaman curry paste
   (see Cook's Tip)
2 tablespoons fish sauce
1 tablespoon palm sugar
4 tablespoons tamarind juice
6 cardamom pods
1 cinnamon stick
8 ounces potatoes, cut into chunks
1 onion, cut into wedges
½ cup roasted peanuts
boiled rice, to serve

1 Bring the coconut milk to a gentle boil in a large saucepan. Add the beef and simmer for about 40 minutes, until tender.

2 Put the coconut cream into a small saucepan. Bring to a boil, then cook for about 5–8 minutes, stirring constantly until it separates.

3 Add the Mussaman curry paste to the coconut cream and cook until fragrant. Then add the fried curry paste to the pan containing the cooked beef.

— COOK'S TIP —

Mussaman curry paste is used to make the Thai version of a Muslim curry. It can be prepared and then stored in a glass jar in the fridge for up to four months.

Remove the seeds from 12 large dried chilies and soak the chillies in hot water for about 15 minutes. Mix 4 tablespoons chopped shallots, 5 garlic cloves, 1 chopped lemongrass stalk, 2 teaspoons chopped galangal, 1 teaspoon cumin seeds, 1 tablespoon coriander seeds, 2 cloves and 6 black peppercorns. Place in a wok and dry-fry over a low heat for 5–6 minutes. Grind or process into a powder and stir in 1 teaspoon shrimp paste, 1 teaspoon salt, 1 teaspoon sugar and 2 tablespoons oil.

4 Add the fish sauce, sugar, tamarind juice, cardamom pods, cinnamon stick, potato chunks and onion wedges. Simmer for 10–15 minutes, or until the potatoes are cooked.

5 Add the roasted peanuts and cook for another 5 minutes. Serve with boiled rice.

Green Beef Curry with Thai Eggplant

This is a very quick curry so be sure to use good quality meat.

INGREDIENTS

Serves 4–6
3 tablespoons vegetable oil
3 tablespoons green curry paste
2½ cups unsweetened coconut milk
1 pound boneless sirloin steak
4 kaffir lime leaves, torn
1–2 tablespoons fish sauce
1 teaspoon palm sugar
5 ounces small Thai eggplant, halved
a small handful of Thai basil
2 green chilies, to garnish

For the green curry paste
15 hot green chilies
2 lemongrass stalks, chopped
3 shallots, sliced
2 garlic cloves
1 tablespoon chopped galangal
4 kaffir lime leaves, chopped
½ teaspoon grated kaffir lime rind
1 teaspoon chopped cilantro root
6 black peppercorns
1 teaspoon coriander seeds, roasted
1 teaspoon cumin seeds, roasted
1 tablespoon sugar
1 teaspoon salt
1 teaspoon shrimp paste (optional)

1 To make the green curry paste, combine all the ingredients except the oil. Pound using a mortar and pestle or process in a food processor until smooth. Add about 2 tablespoons of the oil, a little at a time, blending well. Keep in a jar in the fridge until required.

2 Heat the remaining oil in a large pan. Add 3 tablespoons of the curry paste and fry until fragrant.

3 Stir in half the coconut milk, a little at a time. Cook for about 5–6 minutes, until an oily sheen appears.

4 Cut the beef into long thin slices and add to the saucepan with the kaffir lime leaves, fish sauce, sugar and eggplant. Cook for 2–3 minutes, then stir in the remaining coconut milk.

5 Bring back to a simmer and cook until the meat and eggplant are tender. Stir in the Thai basil just before serving. Finely shred the green chilies and use as a garnish.

Green Shrimp Curry

A popular, fragrant, creamy curry that takes very little time to prepare. It can also be made with thin strips of chicken meat.

INGREDIENTS

Serves 4–6

2 tablespoons vegetable oil
2 tablespoons green curry paste
1 pound jumbo shrimp, shelled
  and deveined
4 kaffir lime leaves, torn
1 lemongrass stalk, bruised
  and chopped
1 cup unsweetened coconut milk
2 tablespoons fish sauce
½ cucumber, seeded and cut into
  thin batons
10–15 basil leaves
4 green chilies, sliced, to garnish

1 Heat the oil in a frying pan. Add the green curry paste and fry until bubbling and fragrant.

2 Add the shrimp, kaffir lime leaves and lemongrass. Fry for 1–2 minutes, until the shrimp are pink.

3 Stir in the coconut milk and bring to a gentle boil. Simmer, stirring occasionally, for about 5 minutes or until the shrimp are tender.

4 Stir in the fish sauce, cucumber and basil, then top with the sliced green chilies and serve.

Pineapple Curry with Shrimp and Mussels

The delicate sweet-and-sour flavor of this curry comes from the pineapple and, although it seems an odd combination, it is rather delicious. Use the freshest shellfish that you can find.

INGREDIENTS

Serves 4–6

2½ cups unsweetened coconut milk
2 tablespoons red curry paste
2 tablespoons fish sauce
1 tablespoon sugar
8 ounces jumbo shrimp, shelled and deveined
1 pound mussels, cleaned and beards removed
6 ounces fresh pineapple, finely crushed or chopped
5 kaffir lime leaves, torn
2 red chilies, chopped, and cilantro leaves, to garnish

1 In a large saucepan, bring half the coconut milk to a boil and heat, stirring, until it separates.

2 Add the red curry paste and cook until fragrant. Add the fish sauce and sugar and continue to cook for a few moments.

3 Stir in the rest of the coconut milk and bring back to a boil. Add the jumbo shrimp, mussels, pineapple and kaffir lime leaves.

4 Reheat until boiling and then simmer for 3–5 minutes, until the shrimp are cooked and the mussels have opened. Remove any mussels that have not opened and discard. Serve garnished with chopped red chilies and cilantro leaves.

Curried Shrimp in Coconut Milk

A curry-like dish where the shrimp are cooked in a spicy coconut gravy.

INGREDIENTS

Serves 4–6

2½ cups unsweetened coconut milk
2 tablespoons yellow curry paste (see Cook's Tip)
1 tablespoon fish sauce
½ teaspoon salt
1 teaspoon sugar
1 pound jumbo shrimp, shelled, tails left intact and deveined
8 ounces cherry tomatoes
juice of ½ lime, to serve
2 red chilies, cut into strips, and cilantro leaves, to garnish

1 Put half the coconut milk into a pan or wok and bring to a boil.

2 Add the yellow curry paste to the coconut milk, stir until it disperses, then simmer for about 10 minutes.

3 Add the fish sauce, salt, sugar and remaining coconut milk. Simmer for another 5 minutes.

4 Add the shrimp and cherry tomatoes. Simmer very gently for about 5 minutes until the shrimp are pink and tender.

5 Serve sprinkled with lime juice and garnished with chilies and cilantro.

COOK'S TIP

To make yellow curry paste, process 6–8 yellow chilies, 1 chopped lemongrass stalk, 4 peeled shallots, 4 garlic cloves, 1 tablespoon peeled chopped fresh ginger, 1 teaspoon coriander seeds, 1 teaspoon mustard powder, 1 teaspoon salt, ½ teaspoon ground cinnamon, 1 tablespoon light brown sugar and 2 tablespoons oil in a blender or food processor. When a paste forms, transfer to a jar and keep in the fridge.

RICE AND NOODLES

A bowl of steamy, fluffy rice is essential to any Thai meal. Rice is a mainstay of Thailand's agriculture and its principal export. It is treated with the greatest of respect.

There are many varieties of rice, but the most commonly used are the white, long grain, fragrant jasmine rice and the large starchy round grain also known as glutinous or sticky rice, which is widely used in making desserts.

After rice, noodles are the second great staple of Oriental kitchens. There are numerous types of noodles and an even greater number of noodle dishes. They make a nutritious and satisfying one-dish meal and are popular for lunch, breakfast or as a snack.

Coconut Rice

This rich dish is usually served with a tangy papaya salad.

INGREDIENTS

Serves 4–6

2 cups jasmine rice
1 cup water
2 cups unsweetened coconut milk
½ teaspoon salt
2 tablespoons sugar
fresh shredded coconut, to garnish
(optional)

1 Wash the rice in several changes of cold water until it runs clear. Place the water, coconut milk, salt and sugar in a heavy-bottomed saucepan.

2 Add the rice, cover, and bring to a boil. Reduce the heat to low and simmer for about 15–20 minutes, or until the rice is tender to the bite and cooked through.

3 Turn off the heat and allow the rice to rest in the saucepan for about 5–10 minutes.

4 Fluff up the rice with chopsticks before serving.

Pineapple Fried Rice

This dish is ideal to prepare for a special occasion meal. Served in the pineapple skin shells, it is certain to be the talking point of the dinner.

INGREDIENTS

Serves 4–6

1 pineapple
2 tablespoons vegetable oil
1 small onion, finely chopped
2 green chilies, seeded and chopped
8 ounces lean pork, cut into
small dice
4 ounces cooked shelled shrimp
3–4 cups cooked cold rice
½ cup roasted cashews
2 scallions, chopped
2 tablespoons fish sauce
1 tablespoon soy sauce
10–12 mint leaves, 2 red chilies, sliced,
and 1 green chili, sliced, to garnish

1 Cut the pineapple in half lengthwise and remove the flesh from both halves by cutting around inside the skin. Reserve the skin shells. You need 4 ounces of fruit, chopped finely (keep the rest for a dessert).

> — COOK'S TIP —
>
> When buying a pineapple, look for a sweet-smelling fruit with an even brownish-yellow skin. To test for ripeness, tap the base – a dull sound indicates that the fruit is ripe. The flesh should also give slightly when pressed.

2 Heat the oil in a wok or large frying pan. Add the onion and chilies and fry for about 3–5 minutes, until softened. Add the pork and cook until it is brown on all sides.

3 Stir in the shrimp and rice and toss well together. Continue to stir-fry until the rice is thoroughly heated.

4 Add the chopped pineapple, cashews and scallions. Season with fish sauce and soy sauce.

5 Spoon into the pineapple skin shells. Garnish with shredded mint leaves and red and green chilies.

Jasmine Rice

A naturally aromatic, long-grain white rice, jasmine rice is the staple of most Thai meals. If you eat rice regularly, you might invest in an electric rice cooker.

INGREDIENTS

Serves 4–6
2 cups jasmine rice
3 cups cold water

COOK'S TIP

An electric rice cooker cooks the rice and keeps it warm. Different sizes and models of rice cookers are available. The top of the range is a nonstick version, which is expensive, but well worth the money.

1 Rinse the rice thoroughly, at least three times, in cold water until the water runs clear.

2 Put the rice in a heavy-bottomed saucepan and add the water. Bring the rice to a vigorous boil, uncovered, over high heat.

3 Stir and reduce the heat to low. Cover and simmer for up to 20 minutes, or until all the water has been absorbed. Remove from the heat and allow to stand for 10 minutes.

4 Remove the lid and stir the rice gently with a rice paddle or a pair of wooden chopsticks, to fluff up and separate the grains.

Fried Jasmine Rice with Shrimp and Thai Basil

Thai basil (*bai grapao*), also known as Holy basil, has a unique, pungent flavor that is both spicy and sharp. It can be found in most Asian food markets.

INGREDIENTS

Serves 4–6
3 tablespoons vegetable oil
1 egg, beaten
1 onion, chopped
1 tablespoon chopped garlic
1 tablespoon shrimp paste
4 cups cooked jasmine rice
12 ounces cooked shelled shrimp
½ cup thawed frozen peas
oyster sauce, to taste
2 scallions, chopped
15–20 Thai basil leaves, coarsely
   chopped, plus an extra sprig,
   to garnish

1 Heat 1 tablespoon of the oil in a wok or frying pan. Add the beaten egg and swirl it around the pan to set like a thin pancake.

2 Cook until golden, slide out on to a board, roll up and cut into thin strips. Set aside.

3 Heat the remaining oil in the wok, add the onion and garlic and fry for 2–3 minutes. Stir in the shrimp paste and mix thoroughly.

4 Add the rice, shrimp and peas and toss together until everything is heated through.

5 Season with oyster sauce to taste, taking great care as the shrimp paste is salty. Add the scallions and basil leaves. Transfer to a serving dish and serve topped with the strips of egg pancake. Garnish with a sprig of basil.

Fried Rice with Pork

If you like, garnish with strips of omelet, as in Fried Jasmine Rice with Shrimp and Thai Basil.

INGREDIENTS

Serves 4–6

3 tablespoons vegetable oil
1 onion, chopped
1 tablespoon chopped garlic
4 ounces pork, cut into small cubes
2 eggs, beaten
4 cups cooked rice
2 tablespoons fish sauce
1 tablespoon dark soy sauce
½ teaspoon superfine sugar
4 scallions, finely sliced, to garnish
2 red chilies, sliced, to garnish
1 lime, cut into wedges and egg omelet, to garnish (optional)

1 Heat the oil in a wok or large frying pan. Add the onion and garlic and cook for about 2 minutes, until softened.

2 Add the pork to the softened onion and garlic. Stir-fry until the pork changes color and is cooked.

3 Add the eggs and cook until scrambled into small lumps.

4 Add the rice and continue to stir and toss, to coat it with the oil and prevent it from sticking.

5 Add the fish sauce, soy sauce and sugar and mix well. Continue to fry until the rice is thoroughly heated. Garnish with sliced scallions, red chilies and lime wedges. If you like, top with a few strips of egg omelet.

Special Chow Mein

Lap cheong is a special air-dried Chinese sausage. It is available from most Chinese markets. If you cannot buy it, substitute with either diced ham, chorizo sausage or salami.

INGREDIENTS

Serves 4–6
3 tablespoons vegetable oil
2 garlic cloves, sliced
1 teaspoon chopped fresh ginger
2 red chilies, chopped
2 lap cheong, about 3 ounces, rinsed
    and sliced (optional)
1 boneless chicken breast, thinly sliced
16 uncooked jumbo shrimp, peeled,
    tails left intact, and deveined
1 cup green beans
1 cup bean sprouts
2 ounces garlic chives
1 pound egg noodles, cooked in
    boiling water until tender
2 tablespoons soy sauce
1 tablespoon oyster sauce
1 tablespoon sesame oil
salt and freshly ground black pepper
2 scallions, shredded, to garnish
1 tablespoon cilantro leaves,
    to garnish

1 Heat 1 tablespoon of the oil in a wok or large frying pan and fry the garlic, ginger and chilies. Add the lap cheong, chicken, shrimp and beans. Stir-fry for about 2 minutes over high heat or until the chicken and shrimp are cooked. Transfer the mixture to a bowl and set aside.

2 Heat the rest of the oil in the same wok. Add the bean sprouts and garlic chives. Stir-fry for 1–2 minutes.

3 Add the noodles and toss and stir to mix. Season with soy sauce, oyster sauce, salt and pepper.

4 Return the shrimp mixture to the wok. Reheat and mix well with the noodles. Stir in the sesame oil. Serve garnished with scallions and cilantro leaves.

Crisp Fried Rice Vermicelli

Mee Krob is usually served at celebratory meals. It is a crisp tangle of fried rice vermicelli, which is tossed in a piquant, garlic, sweet-and-sour sauce.

INGREDIENTS

Serves 4–6
oil for frying
6 ounces rice vermicelli
1 tablespoon chopped garlic
4–6 dried chilies, seeded and chopped
2 tablespoons chopped shallot
1 tablespoon dried shrimp, rinsed
4 ounces ground pork
4 ounces cooked shelled shrimp, chopped
2 tablespoons brown bean sauce
2 tablespoons rice wine vinegar
3 tablespoons fish sauce
3 tablespoons palm sugar
2 tablespoons tamarind or lime juice
½ cup bean sprouts

For the garnish
2 scallions, shredded
2 tablespoons fresh cilantro leaves
2 heads pickled garlic (optional)
2-egg omelet, rolled and sliced
2 red chilies, chopped

1 Heat the oil in a wok. Break the rice vermicelli apart into small handfuls about 3 inches long. Deep-fry in the hot oil until they puff up. Remove and drain on paper towels.

2 Leave 2 tablespoons of the hot oil in the wok, add the garlic, chilies, shallots and shrimp. Fry until fragrant.

3 Add the ground pork and stir-fry for about 3–4 minutes, until it is no longer pink. Add the shrimp and fry for 2 minutes more. Remove the mixture and set aside.

4 To the same wok, add the brown bean sauce, vinegar, fish sauce and palm sugar. Bring to a gentle boil, stir to dissolve the sugar and cook until thick and syrupy.

5 Add the tamarind or lime juice and adjust the seasoning. It should be sweet, sour and salty.

6 Reduce the heat. Add the pork and shrimp mixture and the bean sprouts to the sauce. Stir to mix.

7 Add the rice noodles and toss gently to coat them with the sauce, without breaking the noodles too much. Transfer the noodles to a platter. Garnish with scallions, cilantro leaves, pickled garlic, omelet strips and chilies.

Thai Fried Noodles

Phat Thai has a fascinating flavor and texture. It's made with fine rice noodles and is considered one of the national dishes of Thailand.

INGREDIENTS

Serves 4–6

12 ounces rice noodles
3 tablespoons vegetable oil
1 tablespoon chopped garlic
16 uncooked jumbo shrimp, shelled, tails left intact, and deveined
2 eggs, lightly beaten
1 tablespoon dried shrimp, rinsed
2 tablespoons pickled white radish
2 ounces fried tofu, cut into small slivers
½ teaspoon dried chili flakes
4 ounces garlic chives, cut into 2-inch lengths
1 cup bean sprouts
½ cup roasted peanuts, coarsely ground
1 teaspoon sugar
1 tablespoon dark soy sauce
2 tablespoons fish sauce
2 tablespoons tamarind juice
2 tablespoons cilantro leaves and 1 kaffir lime, to garnish

1 Soak the noodles in warm water for 20–30 minutes, then drain.

2 Heat 1 tablespoon of the oil in a wok or large frying pan. Add the garlic and fry until golden. Stir in the shrimp and cook for about 1–2 minutes, until pink, tossing from time to time. Remove and set aside.

3 Heat another 1 tablespoon of oil in the wok. Add the eggs and tilt the wok to spread them into a thin sheet. Stir to scramble and break the eggs into small pieces. Remove from the wok and set aside with the shrimp.

4 Heat the remaining oil in the same wok. Add the dried shrimp, pickled radish, tofu and dried chilies. Stir briefly. Add the soaked noodles and stir-fry for 5 minutes.

5 Add the garlic chives, half the bean sprouts and half the peanuts. Season with the sugar, soy sauce, fish sauce and tamarind juice. Mix together well and cook until the noodles are completely heated through.

6 Return the shrimp and egg mixture to the wok and mix with the noodles. Serve garnished with the rest of the bean sprouts, peanuts, cilantro leaves and lime wedges.

DESSERTS

Thais, unlike many of their Asian neighbors, consider dessert an essential and harmonious way of rounding off a balanced meal.

Most desserts are based on Thailand's wonderful fruits. The simplest is a platter of fresh tropical fruits, often carved into appealing shapes. Depending on the season, these fruits may include pawpaw, mangoes, custard apple, mangosteen, rambutans, durian and jackfruits. Other fruits, such as banana and pineapple, can be fried in batter to make delicious fritters.

Very often, desserts are eaten between meals as a snack, which explains why some Thai desserts are quite rich and filling.

Coconut milk, an essential ingredient of both savory and sweet dishes, is often incorporated into the dessert menu in one form or another, as in pumpkin stewed with coconut milk, and baked coconut custard.

Tapioca Pudding

This warm pudding, made from large pearl tapioca and coconut milk, is much lighter than the Western-style version. Serve with lychees or the smaller, similar-tasting longans – also known as "dragon's eyes."

INGREDIENTS

Serves 4

²/₃ cup tapioca
2 cups water
scant 1 cup sugar
pinch of salt
1 cup unsweetened coconut milk
9 ounces prepared tropical fruits
finely shredded rind of 1 lime and
   coconut shavings (optional),
   to decorate

1 Soak the tapioca in warm water for 1 hour so the grains swell. Drain.

2 Put the water in a saucepan and bring to a boil. Stir in the sugar and the salt.

3 Add the tapioca and coconut milk and simmer for 10 minutes, or until the tapioca turns transparent.

4 Serve warm with some tropical fruits and decorate with lime rind strips and coconut shavings, if using.

Fried Bananas

These delicious treats are a favorite among children and adults alike. They are sold as snacks throughout the day and night at roadside stalls and market places. Other fruits, such as pineapple and apple, will work just as well.

INGREDIENTS

Serves 4

1 cup all-purpose flour
½ teaspoon baking soda
pinch of salt
2 tablespoons sugar
1 egg
6 tablespoons water
2 tablespoons shredded coconut or
   1 tablespoon sesame seeds
4 firm bananas
oil for frying
2 tablespoons honey, to serve (optional)
sprigs of mint, to decorate

1 Sift the flour, baking soda and salt together into a bowl. Stir in the sugar. Whisk in the egg and add enough water to make the mixture into quite a thin batter.

4 Heat the oil in a wok or deep-frying pan. Dip the bananas in the batter, then gently drop a few into the oil. Fry until golden brown.

2 Whisk in the shredded coconut or sesame seeds.

3 Peel the bananas. Carefully cut each one in half lengthwise, then in half crosswise.

5 Remove from the oil and drain on paper towels. Serve immediately with honey, if using, and decorate with sprigs of mint.

Baked Rice Pudding, Thai-style

Black glutinous rice, also known as black sticky rice, has long black grains and a nutty taste similar to wild rice. This baked pudding has a distinct character and flavor all of its own.

INGREDIENTS

Serves 4–6

6 ounces white or black glutinous (sticky) rice
2 tablespoons light brown sugar
2 cups unsweetened coconut milk
1 cup water
3 eggs
2 tablespoons sugar

1 Combine the glutinous rice, brown sugar, half the coconut milk and all the water in a saucepan.

2 Bring to a boil and simmer for about 15–20 minutes, or until the rice has absorbed most of the liquid, stirring from time to time. Preheat the oven to 300°F.

3 Transfer the rice to one large ovenproof dish or divide it between individual ramekins. Mix together the eggs, remaining coconut milk and sugar in a bowl.

4 Strain and pour the mixture evenly over the par-cooked rice.

5 Place the dish in a baking pan. Pour in enough boiling water to come halfway up the sides of the dish.

6 Cover the dish with a piece of foil and bake in the oven for about 35 minutes to 1 hour, or until the custard is set. Serve warm or cold.

Mango with Sticky Rice

Everyone's favorite dessert. Mangoes, with their delicate fragrance, sweet and sour flavor and velvety flesh, blend especially well with coconut sticky rice. You need to start preparing this dish the day before.

INGREDIENTS

Serves 4

4 ounces glutinous (sticky) white rice
¾ cup thick unsweetened coconut milk
3 tablespoons sugar
pinch of salt
2 ripe mangoes
strips of lime rind, to decorate

1 Rinse the glutinous rice thoroughly in several changes of cold water, then let soak overnight in a bowl of fresh cold water.

2 Drain and spread the rice in an even layer in a steamer lined with cheesecloth. Cover and steam for about 20 minutes, or until the grains of rice are tender.

3 Meanwhile, reserve 3 tablespoons of the top of the coconut milk and combine the rest with the sugar and salt in a saucepan. Bring to a boil, stirring until the sugar dissolves, then pour into a bowl and let cool a little.

4 Turn the rice into a bowl and pour over the coconut mixture. Stir, then let stand for about 10–15 minutes.

5 Peel the mangoes and cut the flesh into slices. Place on top of the rice and drizzle over the reserved coconut milk. Decorate with strips of lime rind.

Coconut Custard

This traditional dish can be baked or steamed, and is often served with sweet sticky rice and a selection of fruit, such as mango and persimmons.

INGREDIENTS

Serves 4–6

4 eggs
6 tablespoons light brown sugar
1 cup unsweetened coconut milk
1 teaspoon vanilla, rose or
    jasmine extract
mint leaves and confectioner's sugar,
    to decorate

1 Preheat the oven to 300°F. Whisk the eggs and sugar in a bowl until they are smooth. Add the coconut milk and vanilla or other extract and blend well together.

2 Strain the mixture and pour into individual ramekins or a cake pan.

3 Stand the ramekins or pan in a roasting pan. Carefully fill the roasting pan with hot water to reach halfway up the outsides of the ramekins or cake pan.

4 Bake for about 35–40 minutes, or until the custards are set. Test with a fine skewer or toothpick.

5 Remove from the oven and cool. Turn out on to a plate, and serve with sliced fruit. Decorate with mint leaves and confectioner's sugar.

Stewed Pumpkin in Coconut Cream

Stewed fruit is a popular dessert in Thailand. Use the firm-textured Japanese kabocha pumpkin for this dish, if you can. Bananas and melons can also be prepared in this way and you can even stew corn kernels or dried beans, such as mung beans and black beans, in coconut milk.

INGREDIENTS

Serves 4–6

2¼ pounds kabocha pumpkin
3 cups unsweetened coconut milk
scant 1 cup sugar
pinch of salt
pumpkin seed kernels, toasted, and
    mint sprigs, to decorate

1 Wash the pumpkin skin and cut off most of it. Scoop out the seeds.

—— COOK'S TIP ——

Any pumpkin can be used for this dessert, as long as it has a firm texture. Jamaican or New Zealand varieties both make good alternatives to kabocha pumpkin.

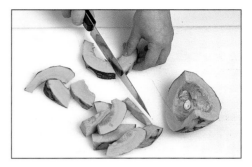

2 Using a sharp knife cut the flesh into pieces about 2 inches long and ¼ inch thick.

3 In a saucepan, bring the coconut milk, sugar and salt to a boil.

4 Add the pumpkin and simmer for 10–15 minutes, until the pumpkin is tender. Serve warm. Decorate each serving with a mint sprig and a few toasted pumpkin seed kernels

Index